Praise for Steve Chapple and *Confessions of an Eco-Redneck*

"Steve Chapple teased the first spring belly-laugh from a long brutal Montana winter. *Confessions of an Eco-Redneck* demonstrates good humor and the wisdom to know that the modern American conservation movement is in real danger from disengagement with the natural world."

> —**Doug Peacock,** author of *Grizzly Years*

"Steve Chapple's *Confessions of an Eco-Redneck* made me laugh and weep in equal measures. How human! I only hope these essays—pungent, knowledgeable, and eminently delightful—can help make the human race stop its silly-ass bickering."

> —**Robert F. Jones,** author of *Tie My Bones to Her Back* and *The Fishing Doctor*

"This red neck is nodding her eco-head back and forth saying, 'Yes! Yes! Yes! And I'll have whatever he's having!' Steve Chapple's *Confessions of an Eco-Redneck* is great. He combines really funny stuff with the prophetic and the true, thereby insuring that every good outdoorsman will think again. Read it."

> —**Rebecca Gray;** Co-founder, *Gray's Sporting Journal* and Contributing Editor, *Sports Afield*

"With wit and insight, Steve Chapple tries to reconcile the red-neck killer and the spirit of Thoreau that divides the hearts of American outdoorsmen. This book is worth reading for the chapter on TV hunting alone."

> —**Phil Caputo,** author of *Equation for Evil* and *A Rumor of War*

"Chapple writes from the edge—and you will never view sport or wildness the same after his shrewd takes on hunting, fly fishing the Zambezi, Bambi, dinosaurs, ecology, marriage, grizzlies, and much "mountain mayhem." He's brilliant, irritating, and uncommonly wise."

> —**Nick Lyons,** author of *A Flyfisher's World*

"Those of us who live shoulder to shoulder with nature truly understand her cycle. *Confessions of an Eco-Redneck* nails the physics of spirituality of our hunting culture."

> —**Ted Nugent,** United Sportsmen of America, latest CD, *Spirit of the Wild*

Confessions of an Eco-Redneck

Or How I Learned to
Gut-Shoot Trout & Save the
Wilderness at the Same Time

Confessions of an Eco-Redneck

Or How I Learned to Gut-Shoot Trout & Save the Wilderness at the Same Time

STEVE CHAPPLE

PLENUM TRADE • NEW YORK AND LONDON

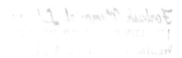

ISBN 0-306-45634-6

© 1997 Steve Chapple
Plenum Press is a Division of Plenum Publishing Corporation
233 Spring Street, New York, N.Y. 10013-1578
http://www.plenum.com

10 9 8 7 6 5 4 3 2 1

Printed in the United States of America

To the memory of Henry A. Chapple, my father

Acknowledgments

I like a good zoo, so long as the animals have room to roam. I'd like to thank some people for opening the gates after dark, and keeping my cages clean at the same time.

Terry McDonell, Sid Evans, and Mike Toth made me look better than I deserve, over there at *Sports Afield*, where hunting and fishing are the Old and New Testaments, only funnier, and wilderness means wild writing. Terry and Sid took sport writing and made it the best of American writing.

Paul Wilner, a good man to have on safari, smart and joyful, seemed to laugh out loud at the ones he published in the *San Francisco Examiner* Magazine. Paul should be locked up—he has too much fun—but it's probably too late now. Julie Just, at the *New York Times*, brought focus to "What Is a River Worth?" Susan Adams and Neil Amdur, also at the *Times*, were kind with "Cheeky Youth—The Mother's Day Caddis Hatch." David McCumber, a true Montanan, let the Yellowstone flow through the first issue of Big Sky *Journal*, and I'm grateful for that.

Erika Goldman, at Plenum, clearly a young woman with the patience of Solomon—though "Let's Return Grizzlies to Central Park" may have to wait for Volume 2—allowed the beast to escape in the first place, and skillfully so. Mary Curioli managed to track me down on two continents.

The Coleman Company kept the campfires burning, over in Africa. Ex Officio made even a bad dresser look elegant in the mud. I was able to wear the same clothes among diplomats and mosquitoes. The Polar-Tek people, who spin fleece from six-pac liners, kept me warm on equatorial nights. Adventure is not cheap.

The rascals, Cody S. and Jack H. D. S. Chapple, crop up from time to time in these pages. I hope they are as kind to their old dad after they learn to read as they are now. I couldn't love them more.

To the Chief Keeper—let's just say it's a good thing Brazilians like writers.

Contents

Confessions of an Eco-Redneck

Or How I Learned to Gut-Shoot Trout & Save the Wilderness at the Same Time

Introduction

Ever since I wandered home to Montana from various urban war zones, I have been writing a series of columns in what folks like to call the sporting press. My first timid outing was titled "TV Hunting in Old Montana," but Terry McDonell, at *Sports Afield,* wisely gave it a more substantial moniker, "Blowing Away the Media," since, clearly, the systematic hunting down of television sets may be the one thing that can save Western civilization from itself.

From gut-shooting TVs, it was on to dinosaurs (dinosaur hunting is a sport that predates the black powder movement), tigerfish, and killer cats. ("Is Mittens with her kittens, or is she outside ripping the lungs from a lark?") And I like house cats.

At the same time that I was writing of clubbing grouse with fishing nets, I was working for more traditional outlets, such as *the New York Times, San Francisco Examiner,* and *Audubon.* These folks, too, would appear to be rethinking soggy ground, which only makes sense. John James Audubon was usually one to eat the birds he painted, soon after he painted them.

In fact, food does not walk onto the plate, in my experience. It has to be killed first.

Even if you yourself don't kill what you eat, somebody else must. Your sister-in-law doesn't find shooting game birds to be a pleasant pastime? Well, has she ever watched cows being sledgehammered at the slaughterhouse? This is what lies behind the waitress's smile.

"I'm a vegetarian!" screams your sister-in-law.

And I can respect that. Vegetarianism will make emotional logic, to vegetarians, until the scientists of the next century play back the tapes of wheat tops screaming under the blades of the thresher.

One man's habitat is another's hunting opportunity.

But I don't hunt or fish simply to put food on the table. I do it because I like to. I love it. I love the endless swirl of water and silence, the smells, the forest, the creatures, life.

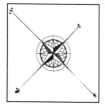 A strange new animal stalks the woods of North America: the eco-redneck. *Ecce homo.* It is an obvious irony to some, an unintentional one to others, but these days sporting persons and environmentalists are apt to be one and the same.

People with graphite fly rods and over-under shotguns are steamed at what is going down in Washington. They want clean water to fish in. They want Mitsubishi and the Canadians off the public lands because deer and little bitty grouse don't like clear-cuts.

The backlash to the backlash has begun.

In the last half decade, 4.1 million Americans have taken up fly-fishing. Several million American women have become shooters of pheasant and deer. (Men may be from Mars, but women still prefer 30.06s.) Wilderness, what is left of it, can be fun, properly clothed.

Just what is an eco-redneck? Hard to tell sometimes, at least for me, because in Montana the sun rarely gets hot enough to pink a neck properly. An eco-redneck likes to hug trees. But he may be just primitive enough to punch your lights out if you try to embarrass him.

I like to think this book has as much truth in it

as lies, but I'm not a stickler. "It is not worthwhile to strain one's self to tell the truth to people who habitually discount everything you tell them, whether it is true or isn't," Mark Twain wrote in his *Autobiography*, and I agree, though I happen to agree more with Leonard Cohen, when he sings: "I don't give a damn for the truth, baby, except, perhaps, for the naked truth."

Actually, telling the truth has always gotten me into trouble as a writer.

It has not been all huckleberries, moving back to Montana, just as it has not been all trophy browns reacquainting myself with the trout in the Madison, the Gallatin, and the Yellowstone (please see "Tackling Life," though the paragraph about the California woman who pierces her nipples with #14 Royal Coachman trout flies may not be for everyone. Or then again, it probably is.)

I fervently hope this front-loaded collection of mountain mayhem, fishy politics, and shotgun attacks on defenseless Trinitrons will be seen as a polite addition to American letters. Naturally, I'd also like to think that the work will contribute to a deeper understanding of the times we are in, that it will cut through the cant, scatter the ballyho, spear the ferrets, and speak to that genetic yearning for the spiritual through blood sport that lies deep within the hindbrain of us all. I know that a careful reading of the text will teach the more adept among you how to tie a pig's tail with your tongues.

Thank you for your time.

Rods to the ready.

Steve Chapple
Pray, Montana

Eco-Rednecks

It was the best fishing I've had in Montana. Every cast, whether perfect lay or clumsy drag upon the water, anything we threw—popper, hopper, or coachman—garnered a strike, until we were laughing in victory and sweating with the effort. Turned out, the reason it was so good was that it was the Saturday before fishing season opened. The fish had no idea we were breaking the law.

In my defense, I was only 10. My friend's mother had driven us up the Stillwater for a day's easy baby-sitting, and she was not, looking back on it, such a punctilious sportswoman.

Neither was her husband. He took us trolling on Yellowstone Lake in the park a little later in the summer. Soon enough, using red and white daredevils, we were more than a little over the limit and—exciting moment!—a patrol boat set out from the marina to check up on us.

"Empty the freezer!" shouted my friend's father. We kids tossed 30 or 40 dead cutthroats over the transom.

Then the great helmsman crisscrossed the Evinrude over the floating trout until they were, at best, chum. When the patrol boat drew alongside, he voluntarily threw open the cooler. He was a cocky bastard.

"You're one over," said the ranger, after counting.

"They were really biting!" explained my friend's father.

The ranger let us off.

The souls of those salmonids still weigh on my conscience, I guess. Today, we'd call my friend's father a game hog, maybe even a redneck, though in Montana, the sun never gets hot enough to pink a neck properly. As I recall, my friend's father had to open his mouth to spit, so he could not have been an authentic redneck, anyway.

At bottom, he was a meat hunter, devil take the hindquarters, catch and fillet. Nothing wrong with that, either—once you factor out excessive zeal—because food does not walk onto the plate, in my experience. It has to be killed first.

Even if you yourself don't kill what you eat, somebody else must. Your sister-in-law doesn't find shooting game birds to be a pleasant pastime? Well, has she ever watched cows being sledgehammered at the slaughterhouse? This is what lies behind the waitress's smile.

"I'm a vegetarian!" screams your sister-in-law.

And I can respect that. Vegetarianism will make emotional logic, to vegetarians, until the scientists of the next century play back the tapes of wheat tops screaming under the blades of the thresher.

Even then, there can be no difference, in the eyes of the Lord, between mycorrhiza soil bacteria and an elk steak. You walk, you step on beetles. It's kill or be killed, and let God sort out the giblets.

But how did we get to this pass? How have the small number of anti-hunters and those who eschew steak tartar come to be identified as environmentalists, and those of us who trout-box for breakfast and prefer antelope medallion to acorn souffle (which is not bad, actually) come to be imagined as unconcerned for the land?

It defies common sense. Who loves the mountains more than those who hunt them? Who has done more for wetlands than duck hunters? More to stop nickel-and-dime trailer courts, subdivisions, and septic tanks at streamside than trout and bass organizations? More to convince farmers not to rainforest-torch the cover that runs alongside country roads than pheasant beaters? Those who enjoy tying into the bull trout, that tiger shark of the northern Rockies, are learning that acid mine waste must be stopped in the headwaters, because the bulls are like prize-fighters with bad lungs. They can't stand even minimal pollution.

These days, sportsman and environmentalist are apt to be the same person. There is a strange new animal stalking the woods of North America: the eco-redneck.

Of course, there is nothing new about eco-rednecks, really, except for the name. John James Audubon often shot and ate the birds he drew, as I've said. ("So we took our guns and went after Black-breasted Lark Buntings," *The Missouri River Journals*, 1843.) The two main founders of the modern conservation movement were forester Aldo Leopold, an avid hunter of deer along New Mexico's Gila, and, of course, Teddy "Hunting Trips of a Ranchman" Roosevelt: "The whitetail . . . keeps its place in the land in spite of the swinish game-butchers, who hunt for hides and not for sport or actual food, and who murder the gravid doe and the spotted fawn with as little hesitation as they would kill a buck of ten points. No one who is not himself a sportsman and lover of nature can realize the intense indignation—"

Whoa, Theodore!

I think what happened is some thoroughbred rednecks got control of the White House after the first Roosevelt and sullied the waters, which confused our minds. Consider this quote from a recent official of the Department of Interior: "If you can't shoot it, hook it, or screw it, it's not worth conserving." What's wrong with this is not elegance of prose. I like a direct speaker, always an endangered species inside the Beltway. The problem is snail-darters make good bait, spotted owls are a sign of a healthy forest, and if we don't let small-scale controlled burns put back forbs and grass at the edge of conifer forests, we won't have elk to shoot come fall. You see, in Washington, they're always willing to cut the forests to save the tees.

That, bottom line, may be why sportsmen and environmentalists are too often kept on opposite sides of the barbed wire: so they won't see how close they really are to each other.

Right now there is even a scheme afoot to chainsaw the cottonwoods along western rivers and mill them into coffins. A writer couldn't ask for a more perfect metaphor. In turn for caulking the juices of dead folks, countless bobcats, raccoons, whitetails, bald eagles, and rabbits will have to look elsewhere for homes, which they will not find, and the denuded banks of the streams and rivers themselves will erode faster than a hemophiliac's scab.

An eco-redneck is not ashamed to hug a tree. But he may be just primitive enough to punch out your lights if you try to embarrass him.

What does the proper eco-redneck dress like? Over his folding knife and his bag of urine gel powder (which masks his scent) he probably wears one of those new fleece pullovers made from recycled soft-drink containers. He prefers his petrol-garb in camo green, but he won't be truly happy until the Polar-Tek people come up with a way to spin fleece directly from crushed beer cans

Like life itself, it all comes back to food and drink—or to the eco-redneck, to quail breast in a butter cognac sauce with a cold Bud beside the plate.

Cheeky Youth
The Mother's Day
Caddis Hatch

When aquatic insects metamorphose from bottom-crawling larvae into winged flies and lift off the surface of the water, anglers call it a hatch. There are famous mayfly hatches on the Beaverkill and Willowemoc rivers in New York, on Fishing Creek in Pennsylvania, and on Hat Creek in northern California. But perhaps the most legendary—if not the most holy—fly-fishing event in the country is the Mother's Day caddis hatch on the Yellowstone River, near the little trout-daft cowboy town of Livingston, Montana, 60 miles north of Yellowstone Park.

The caddis hatch on the Yellowstone is a moment of such religious frenzy for rainbow and German brown trout that anglers, both local and those who have made the pilgrimage from out of state, are often themselves driven buggy.

In a good year, the plain but tasty caddis flies may rise off the river by the millions in clouds that blanket rocks and streamside willows and infiltrate clothing, hair, and tackle. Trout that are normally wary commit indiscretions, boiling to the surface in unguarded haste to catch the bugs before they vanish into the big sky. Sober river guides wax poetically of "floating caddis rafts" and "blizzard hatches." The usual gentle angler may turn incautious with greed.

There is only so much time. The brief blitz of caddis flies presents a small window of opportunity. The hatch is triggered by rising water temperatures that coincide with lengthening spring days. But warmer temperatures soon melt the snow pack in the Absaroka and Gallatin mountains, above the Yellowstone, and the river can rise quickly, sometimes 2 or 3 feet overnight, and turn muddy and un-fishable. Locals call this a blowout. It is a sort of catch-22.

Mother's Day 1994, I was flailing the swirl from a rocky point just south of Carter's Bridge at the entrance to Paradise Valley, a scoop of Himalayan grandeur and vacation homes just below town. Geese and coots called to each other in the slack water behind me, and osprey perched in the cottonwoods above. But I saw only the river in front of me. Each cast I made, inept or elegant, resulted in a hookup. Sometimes the fish were large, 18 to 20 inches. Smaller trout I tried to shake off. All across the knifing eddies, hundreds more broke the surface. In this stretch of the Yellowstone, which is possibly the most productive on the river, there are as many as 2500 trout to the mile. Though no innocent, I was in such a state of giddy hysteria I soon forgot to pay much attention to my back cast.

I heard a scream. I turned around. I had hooked my 4-year-old son in the cheek. That is, the hook had entered his mouth and got stuck on the inside. He was a brave little boy. He didn't cry, probably from the shock of it. There was a trickle of blood. His mother dropped her fly rod and rushed over.

We drove quickly to the emergency room. The irony of a father hooking his son during the Mother's Day caddis hatch was not lost on me (or on my wife.) The Park Street Clinic in Livingston is located on the river, beside the 9th Street Bridge. Thousands of caddis flies batted against the windows as we waited. The doctor introduced himself. He popped open my son Jack's cheek with a gloved finger, gingerly.

"Number 14 Parachute Adams," the doctor pronounced. "Am I right?"

We had come to the right place. With a hank of

what looked like dental floss, the doctor lassoed the Parachute Adams, a caddis imitation, and extracted its pinched barb without a whimper from Jack, though his mother was about ready to faint. For my part, I was relieved. There was still a good hour of fishing time before sunset. Back at Carter's Bridge, I let Jack pull in the next trout.

This year, a few days ago, on Thursday, I called up river guide Chester Marion, who had caught the largest brown trout of the decade, an 11-pound, 11-ounce German brown, in April of 1994, not so far from Carter's Bridge. The trout's picture, along with Marion's, had appeared on the front page of the Livingston *Enterprise* under a huge pull quote that read: "I've been on a collision course with this fish for 40 years."

Actually, Marion told me, as we drove south to Mallard's Rest, a picture postcard fishing access near where the dance scene in *A River Runs through It* was filmed, he had been guiding the Yellowstone for over 42 years.

"I am the best," he said. "The rest are amateurs." He laughed. "I am not a modest man."

Marion, 59, had also taught senior high school English for 13 years in Livingston. I asked him what his favorite texts had been.

"The Bible, both Testaments, and *Big Two-Hearted River,* by Hemingway," he said without hesitation.

Marion, a short, strong, purposeful man, never seemed to hesitate. He moved the 14½-foot Lavro drift boat off its trailer and into the current at Mallard's Rest like a bull moving in a pen.

"There's a lone caddis," he said, pointing to an inch-long brown bug hovering beside a budding poplar. The caddis larva is even more homely than the winged adult. The larvae disguise themselves beneath sand and little sticks and are best described, in *Sports Afield Trout Fisher's Almanac,* as resembling a wet cat, only smaller.

Into the gunwales of the boat we loaded the proper tackle, an 8-foot graphite rod, which Marion had made himself, equipped with a Hardy Princess reel, pink 444 Cortland weight-forward #6 fly line, a 3X tippet (the tapered monofilament that joins floating fly line to hook), and a #14 elk hair caddis from Dan Bailey's Fly Shop in town.

"We're just going through the motions, here," said Marion, a bit disgusted. The game plan had been to launch his boat, the *Tippy Spruce,* row quickly to the other side, and wade fish in the vicinity where he had hooked the 11-pound, 11-ounce German brown in 1994. But in the night, the Yellowstone had risen wickedly and had muddied up, dark as a catfish fried in paprika. It was over.

Marion showed me pages from his river diary, which he had brought along. I copied the entry from 1984, a peak year: "May 3–9th (*700 trout approx.) (1) Perhaps the fastest week of dryfly fishing I've ever seen—for fish up to 18"—the brown on 5/9 was 21"; (2) 5/6—Sunday—over 125 fish on nymphs & dries; (3) 5/4—heaviest hatch of caddis (any kind of flies) I've ever seen—literally covered the water."

For me, it was like reading Bluebeard's treasure map.

Marion said that the Mother's Day caddis hatch was cyclical. "As a blizzard hatch, it really got its start in the 1980s, '83 or '84, when agricultural fertilizers were developed that weren't so toxic to fish, along with softer sprinkling systems that didn't flood the river's banks. Word got out. I counted 55 drift boats at Carter's in 1986."

Marion shook his head at the number.

I had talked the night before to Richard Parks, of Park's Fly Shop in Gardiner, Montana, where the Yellowstone leaves Yellowstone Park. Parks told me that in the 1950s, the Mother's Day caddis hatch had arrived earlier, in mid-April, and had been called, simply, "The Caddis Hatch, or as I termed it, 'The Resurrection Hatch.'" In 1955, according to Parks, the United States Forest Service, in an attempt to eradicate the spruce bud worm, had sprayed the Yellowstone River, as well as nearby forests, with DDT, an incident logged in Rachael Carson's book *Silent Spring.*

"It was like killing flies with a sledgehammer," said Parks. "Trout and whitefish died by the thousands, after ingesting DDT-killed bugs. The mink were wiped out, and the eagles were hurt bad. The consequences have been ricocheting through the ecosystem ever since. The caddis hatch has taken decades to recover."

Mr. Parks, Mr. Marion, and other veteran river guides point out that the record high waters of 1996 may also have affected the caddis hatch. "The big flood of last year crushed their little bodies," the guide Dan Lahren said, "and the resulting shallow sheet ice of the winter may have croaked the bugs for a year or two."

"Enough caddis survived to keep the species alive," said Tim Williams of Dan Bailey's Fly Shop, "but not enough to get in your underwear, at least this year."

Along the Yellowstone, trout fishers are sad but hopeful. The Mother's Day caddis hatch has always been a gentlemen's affair, for all its religious frenzy.

"I've never seen it start before 10 or 11 on a given day," Lahren said, "and usually 1 is about right."

This suits the Livingston style of angler just fine. Jimmy Buffett wrote the popular song "Livingston Saturday Night" here. Bars close late in Montana. Plenty of time to sleep in, with buggy dreams.

The Bambi Syndrome

IDYLLIC FOREST SCENE
(Three shots ring out!)
BAMBI
(Voice-over)
We made it, Mother! Mother? Mother?
Where are you, Mother?
(Long silence—4 beats)
GREAT PRINCE OF THE FOREST
(Sonorously)
Your Mother can't be with you any more, Bambi.
Come with me, son.

Not a dry eye in the house! Least of all mine, and I filled two Doe B Tags last year.

To quote Roger Ebert, of two thumbs-up fame, "In the annals of the great heartbreaking moments in the movies, the death of Bambi's mother ranks right up there with the chaining of Mrs. Jumbo and the moment when E.T. seems certainly dead."

Of course, there's a couple things wrong with the scene, which, if you have ever bought a hunting license, may jump out at you. First is that, at this point in the movie, Bambi is a spotted fawn. Somebody, identified only as "Man," is shooting at deer considerably younger than "antlerless." Also, it's the dead of winter. These nameless poachers are poaching out of season, even.

I realize holding up *Bambi* to the lamp of truth is like asking if Mother Teresa takes bribes, but *Bambi*, the movie, has probably formed the image of hunting for more children in America than any other piece of media distortion. I call it "The Bambi Syndrome."

Whenever Man the Hunter enters Bambi's forest, he sprays bullets at chipmunks, skunks, songbirds, Thumper, anything that moves, including a blind mole that makes the mistake of sticking its head above ground, in such a blood lust of poorly aimed slob hunting that it makes Udel Hussein, who is on record for hunting ducks with an Uzi, look like a beginner in hunter safety class. Then Man the Hunter torches the set, or forest, with a carelessly contained campfire. After a few *Bambi* viewings, talking to the kids about God's cycle of death, Ortega y Gasset on hunting, or even putting dinner on the table is an uphill battle.

Now don't get me wrong. I believe *Bambi* is a great movie, and I'm pleased to see that it has been rereleased, with the usual happy fanfare. *Bambi* is about the seasons of life, about growing up, falling in love, bonding with your dad, respecting your mom, locking horns with your rivals, and, not least, the intense drama of the rut. As a movie, *Bambi*'s got it all. The part where the young hero gets twitterpated and defends the honor of Faline's venison against the challenge of the darkly evil Ronno, and afterward they go for a ramble in the Disney brambles, well, this is the stuff of a director's cut.

But Hollywood has a problem with hunting.

"I use antlers in all my decorating," yells Gaston, the handsome blunderbuss-toting cretin who hankers after Belle's own bookish venison in *Beauty and the Beast.* You might not know, if you saw *Fly Away Home,* that millions of acres of wetland in the United States were saved by duck and goose hunters. And I hate to think what *101 Dalmatians* (without a doubt Glenn Close's finest role) has done for the honored profession of taxidermy. But it is not good.

Let's delve deeper. Has anyone ever read the

book *Bambi,* written by one Felix Salten? To Salten, Bambi's forest was a pretty scary place:

> It was silent in the woods, but something horrible happened every day. Once the crows fell upon Friend Hare's small son who was lying sick and killed him in a cruel way. He could be heard moaning pitifully for a long while. Friend Hare was not at home, and when he heard the sad news he was beside himself with grief. Another time the squirrel raced about with a great wound in his neck where the ferret had caught him. . . . He ran about for an hour, then suddenly crumpled up, fell across a branch, and dropped dead in the snow. A couple of magpies flew down at once to begin their meal. . . . Another day a fox tore to pieces the strong and handsome pheasant who had enjoyed such general respect and popularity. . . . No one could have felt safer than the pheasant for it all happened in broad daylight. The terrible hardship that seemed to have no end spread bitterness and brutality. It destroyed all their memories of the past, their faith in each other, and ruined every good custom they had. There was no longer peace or mercy in the forest.

This is kid's stuff? Salten, whose book was translated by Whittaker Chambers in 1929, the foreword written by British Nobel prize-winner John Galsworthy, was driven out of Germany by the Nazis and eventually died in Switzerland. *Bambi* had a lot of dark adult undertones, before Walt got hold of it, and Salten later wrote an even more explicit allegory of good and fascist evil called *Fifteen Rabbits,* which makes *Watership Down* play like *The Shaggy Dog*, which, no kidding, was originally a lighter Salten opus called *Der Hund von Florenz* (*The Hound of Florence*).

All of this helps explain why *Bambi* is such a powerful film. Salten had more on his mind than deer; those Hunters were breathing down his neck, too. Even so, he comes across a little morbid, a bleeding heart of a European intellectual. I mean, *"The terrible hardship that seemed to have no end spread bitterness and brutality."* Don't ferrets have a right to life, too? And what's a magpie supposed to do? Not eat carrion?

In Hollywood there's this pathetic, romantic inability to call a spade a spade, to deny the naked lunch at the end of the fork, to create Bad Guys when all we're talking about here is life and nature, and then, after the story conference ends, to blithely order out for Kung Pao beef, that has led Hollywood to vilify hunting and hunters. Hollywood confuses deer hunting with *The Deer Hunter,* the idea that if you want to quit killing your fellow man, you've got to first stop killing animals.

But what do I know? I know I believe in cinema verité, so I put in a few calls to L.A., the better to understand myth creation. First, I ring up Terry Curtin, senior vice president of publicity at Disney. While on hold, I am treated to a tape of Goofy singing about Christmas. I wait long enough to guess that Ms. Curtin does not often get calls from the sporting press.

"What's this in regard to?" an assistant finally asks.

"Well, you know, there's about 20 million hunters in America, and Disney just rereleased *Bambi,* and you did *The Lion King* and *Beauty and the Beast,* and

I just wanted to ask Ms. Curtin a couple questions about Hollywood's attitude toward blood sport—"

"I will give her the message that you called," says the assistant. It takes me half a minute to realize the conversation is over.

Well, anyone who has managed to fill two Doe B Tags does not give up so easily. I had seen a picture of Sherry Lansing in an ad for American Express cards, and I knew she ran Paramount and that Paramount had made *The Ghost in the Darkness*, with Val Kilmer and Michael Douglas, definitely a pro-hunting picture, unless you happen to be a lion, and maybe even then. Ms. Lansing is momentarily unavailable, but her assistant puts me immediately in touch with *Ghost's* publicist, Allen Burry.

"*The Ghost in the Darkness*," I begin tactfully, "was a great movie. Does this mean hunting is becoming fashionable in Hollywood, like cigars?"

"How would I know?" replies Burry. "I live in Los Angeles. I don't think I know anyone who hunts. You live in Montana. You must be surrounded by that sort of thing."

Then Michael Douglas, or somebody, gets on another line, and I guess our conversation is over.

But since I now had an in at Paramount, I called up Lansing's office again. "Can you give me William Goldman's number?" Goldman wrote *The Ghost and the Darkness*, also *Butch Cassidy & the Sundance Kid*, and a few other bloody epics I enjoyed.

"He's on location."

"How about John Milius?"

I admit, Milius never really wrote an explicitly all-hunting picture, but he directed *Conan the Barbarian*, and he came up with Robert Duvall's line in *Apocalypse Now* —"I love the smell of napalm in the morning!"—which I loved, and I had heard he was a gun nut, so that seems close enough. I don't want to push my luck; I'm already chatting with the head of Paramount, her office at least. Anyway, they give me Milius's number.

I call. No answer. I figure the philosopher is out shooting frogs, or something.

I need some answers, though. Deadline pressure. I remember a friend, Gatz Hjortsberg, who had written 20 contracted screenplays, even wrote the first draft to *A River Runs through It.*

"How'd you happen to do *A River Runs through It?*" I ask Gatz when I catch up with him at his apartment in San Francisco.

"That was 25 years ago," he says. "The president of Paramount was a fly fisherman then, and he figured if he green-lighted *River,* he could at least spend the summer fishing. He got canned, for something else, and my screenplay became more evidence of his madness. Who would pay money to watch a movie about trout?"

My friend is in a good mood, I think, because in Hollywood if they don't like something you do, they still pay you for it.

"You can shoot humans to death on the screen in all sorts of creative, horrible ways," he says. "But you cannot kill a real animal. That's bottom line. Period. I suppose you could use robotic elk in the hunting scenes, maybe. You know in *Unforgiven,*" he said, "English Bob was blasting computer pheasants, I think it was, and pheasants of any kind hadn't even been introduced to the American West, at the time. Nobody in Hollywood has anything against hunting. That's hunter paranoia. Whatever political sensibilities are currently bankable, as defined by market research, which means what flies for a bunch of bored teenagers on an odd Saturday night in a test theater in Orange County, that's what get's made."

Kind of makes me wonder how an anti-fascist allegory like *Bambi* ever got filmed.

But my last call is to John Veitch, the producer of *Fly Away Home.* "Sure," he says, "you come up with a good story wrapped around hunting, and we'll take a look at it."

So I'm working on this script about a Montana writer and his best friend, a bowie knife. The writer runs down buck deer in his bare feet, slits their throats in the snow. Then, he hooks up with this rather gorgeous Italian anti-fur crusader. Then the aliens from Mars attack—

I don't have the ending yet.

But I have the contacts.

Fly-Fishing the
Zambezi

> The tigerfish of Africa is the fiercest fish that
> swims. Let others hold forth as advocates for the
> mako shark, the barracuda, the piranha of the
> Amazon, or the bluefish of the Atlantic. To them I
> say, "Pish and tush!"
> —Leander J. McCormick, *Game Fish of the World*

It looked like a good place for tigers. Certainly, there were plenty of elephants. A herd of 12 crashed into the Zambezi a quarter mile upstream from me, trumpeting and spraying each other like mad bathers at a skinny-dipping party. Much closer, two Cape buffalo chewed their cuds and contemplated gore. (Buffalo, as the ancients say, always look at you as if you owed them money—a lot of money.) I laid my first cast close to shore, in a pocket below a swirl of white water, and waited, patiently, for my arms to be ripped off.

It was not the first time I had gone angling for tigerfish along the Zambezi. A year before and 400 miles upriver, on a loco raft trip down the world's biggest white water, which thrashes through the Batoka Gorge to form the border between Zimbabwe and Zambia, I had brought along a fly rod and a couple of Bitch Creek nymphs from Bozeman, in order better to unwind from the ripples at day's end. I had seen a mounted tiger in the gift shop at the Meikles Hotel in Harare, and the thing looked like a cross between a 10-pound barracuda and a wolverine with interlocking teeth. A tiger can accelerate to 110 kilometers/hour in under five seconds. Which is fast. It dines on anything up to a third its own size, including younger brothers, daughters, and small crocodiles, and when the tiger strikes, none other than the official Keeper of Angling Records for Zimbabwe, Harold Voss, had told me, it feels like a fat man hitting you between the shoulders.

So I was intrigued, back-casting away the opalescent orange sunsets after rafting, when the African fish eagles scream like ravens faking pain, and we waited for the Zambezi Slammers (gin, filtered river water, and Gatorade) to be shaken for our rustic enjoyment by the pale Sobek guides. These guides were mostly from northern California, and made a cocktail as functional as any served at John's Grill on Ellis Street.

But that first time out, in terms of tigerfish, I guess I got skunked. Perhaps the Batoka Gorge was too fast or too deep to hold bait fish, or perhaps I was always paying more attention to my feet and what might be nibbling at them than to my back cast. The gorge harbored some large crocodiles, 10- to 15-footers, though not nearly so many as here in the Mana Pools stretch, downriver.

I made another cast. For my second trip to Africa, I had left the fly rod at home and rashly purchased a little Shakespeare Ultra-Lite, since I thought bait-fishing might be the ticket, for tigers. I was using balls of ostrich meat, leftovers packed from the Ilala Lodge in Victoria Falls, and I had also optimistically loaded the tiny reel with outsized 12-pound test monofilament.

The elephants quieted down. The nearby buffalo edged away. Two casts. No strikes. I was already disappointed. This was not the Beartooths at ice-out.

Suddenly, I heard shouting. It was Victor Neube, my Zulu guide. The dawn had brought up the wind, and the tents, half-struck, were blowing away. I set the pole down in the sand and ran to gather my own tent before it draped the horns of a water buffalo.

Some may think it unwise to leave a pole on the ground, line in the water, when fishing for the world's most ferocious game fish. These folks would be about right.

I recovered the tent, packed it in its stuff bag, and returned to the bank. My outfit was gone. Victor strolled over. He was a fully licensed guide, one of only seven Afro-African guides in Zimbabwe, a former major in the liberation struggle, a man who had saved my hiney a couple of times without even trying, and probably a couple of more times without bothering to tell me, but even Victor had never followed the tracks of a spinning rod into deep water.

We both stared over the bank.

I could tell Victor thought wading after the rig would be a real dumb idea.

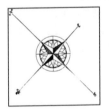

To find them in large numbers generally requires a visit to alarming and out-of-the-way locales.
—Leander J. McCormick, *Game Fish of the World*

The third time I encountered the world's most ferocious game fish was in a more formal setting. The tents were anchored, and we had what are called *en suite* bathrooms, meaning that after you unzipped the double malaria nets, you were still under the canopy of an acacia tree, and there was a hanging canvas bucket shower filled each night by non-California camp helpers with good hot water.

"Tiger Camp," as it was mysteriously named,

was so alarmingly out of the way, located on the Barotse flood plain in the middle upper Zambezi, in Zambia, where the Lozi used to consecrate a good canoe with the blood from the fingers of a captured child, that I did not realize it at first, until a freshly painted brand-new twin-engined white Cessna with no markings roared over our heads at treetop level, which on the flood plain, where there are few trees, was about 30 feet.

"About two times a week," shrugged Nathan, as he helped to set the drag on my boat rod, "that plane flies into Angola, comes back. I think it has a base in the Indian Ocean. Brings in guns, takes out diamonds. They don't respond to our radio calls. Costs a lot of money to run a plane like that, place like this. Take care when the tiger strikes, pull from the side, not up, like some marlin, that encourages them to jump, shake the lure."

Nathan dropped the boat into trolling speed. He was a white kid, 19, went to school in London, wanted to start a rose plantation in Africa, already had some backers. "All's you need is about $600,000 American. Double your money in 2, 3 years." Nathan lit a cigarette, steered wide around a couple of narrow dugouts loaded with bags of mealie-meal, the polers casting tall shadows across the far shore.

I checked the drag. They're professional, in the middle of nowhere, Daiwa S130s, 6.1:1, Telstar Fire-Stiks, 15-kilogram line. Before, while Nathan was getting the boat ready, I had stood on the rocky point below the dock with a 9-weight fly rod, floating line, and an LSD streamer, a punked-out mess of dyed hackles so named for its vibrant colors, the most popular fly on this section of the Zambezi. A couple of tiger dinks in the 4- or 5-pound class frogged across the top of the water, their mouths open like early morning drunks. They whacked the fly as if, next strike, it would be my kidneys. They got their message across, those little guys. We were not about to go walleye fishing.

Nathan called out, as I started back across the rocky point for the dock, "Mind the water!"

I stepped away from the bank. Nathan explained that a few years back, six women, at different times, had been swept off the rocks by one particularly adroit crocodile. Starting deep and gathering speed, the croc had broken the surface with a skidding slide, tail curled—thus was his terrible modus operandi—and thwacked the women, who had been washing clothes, into the gentle swirl, where they could be dined upon at leisure.

A policeman was brought up from Lukulu. The croc charged him, too, but the cop pulled out a shotgun and blew the reptile away. Even so, the entire village moved inland, citing bad *muti.* The chief of the Lozi, which is like saying the governor of Nebraska, granted an easement to the Tiger Camp people, though the locals still found it strange anyone would pay to hunt tigerfish, which are a bit bony, even boiled.

In the beginning, the camp's tagging procedures were regarded with skepticism by some. It was believed the fish were being implanted with diamond-seeking electronics. Bush planes were viewed with cross-cultural curiosity. One of the first, a King Air from Johannesburg, was surrounded by a crowd of 300 folks shouting "Donafish! Donafish!" A donafish is a mermaid. Rumor was, a mermaid was inside the parked plane, hidden by the sun shield. As the King Air was about to be rocked like a Mercedes in a riot, a soldier ran onto the tarmac and yelled: "The donafish has gone to the river to mate a donaman!" Nat-

51

urally, the crowd dispersed for the river. I would have, too.

On the boat, we began trolling. I was thinking of what had happened to an angler earlier in the season. He was fighting a thin-faced bream on light tackle when a tiger rushed his fish. The bream jumped out of the water, only to be grabbed by a fish eagle. But then the eagle dropped the bream. The bream, still hooked, was landed and tagged. I decided even panfish are hardy, in Africa.

Anyway, when my own reel began to scream, we were passing an assemblage of open-billed storks under an ilala palm. The storks were clacking about something, something important, I'm sure. I grabbed the rod and struck with the tip up. That stick rattled my bones. Hemingway has a line about fishing off Cuba, where he says if the fisherman had a hook in his mouth, or his jaw, or in his stomach which was attached to the gear he was playing the fish with, and on which pressure would be exerted comparable to that put on the fish, then the term *fight* might be applied. Equal and mortal combat. I was glad Hemingway was not a game warden on the Zambezi.

The tiger charged out of the water and tail-walked toward the boat. I cranked madly. He dove. I pulled straight up, doing everything wrong. The tiger jumped again, shook his head like an Airedale with a rat. At least the lure did not hit us in the face as it whizzed past.

"Nice fish, that one," said Nathan.

Nathan kept a record of screw-ups. Only one in five tigers hooked was ever brought to transom. The mouth of a tigerfish is armor-plated, like a mako's, only more so, and the jaws are articulated with a hinge up front, like a nutcracker, so that the back can be made bigger, at will. Piranhas, which are related to tigerfish, have somewhat the same mechanism, which allows them to swallow large prey. A tiger's jaws are also worked with unusually strong muscles, and the mouth has two rows of teeth. When the tiger hits, it merely clamps down on the spoon like one of those twirling circus performers who holds the end of the rope in her teeth. The hook rarely penetrates the tiger's mouth. It is there at the discretion of the fish, and when the fish is done playing with the angler, it spits the shiny metal trash out and goes back to the more serious business of attacking other tigerfish and unwary small crocodiles. The only way to hook a tiger is from the side, where the point has a better chance of piercing, or to foul hook it.

So the next time a wily tiger masticated the drone, about 15 minutes upstream, I just about thrust the end of the rod in the river and struck from underwater.

The funny thing is, the tigerfish fights so hard, by the time it is brought to boat, it is usually spent. Nathan took this one off the hook as if it were a kitten and ran its 4-kilogram body up and down in the current, gently, to help it recover. It did not. He laid it in the boat. I stared at the eyes. They did not look fishy. With a black pupil and a yellow iris, they looked more like a bobcat's. Though dead (said Nathan) the fish kept opening and shutting its mouth. Gnashing its disembodied teeth for the short journey to tiger hell, you could say. But, to me, there was a strange sadness in those eyes. Unfishlike. It was as if I had killed a coyote or a bear. More than that. This fish was primeval. Its adipose fin even had a couple of bony stubby legs positioned below it. Once it had walked upon land. Now it was dead, this specimen at least. I knew what Leander J. Mc-

Cormick would say: "Bwana, you have been under an African sun too long. Grill the sucker before he grills you."

I was, I realized, locking into those yellow tiger eyes, far from home, on the Zambezi. Good-night gringos and sayanora senoritas.

Pish and tush.

Killer Cats

Cats are not necessarily the cuddly house pets we have all come to know and stroke. They are small tigers, and they are decimating the game and song-birds of the earth—pheasants, finches, even swallows, which have been observed caught in mid-air by particularly bold tabbies leaping from the roofs of farm outbuildings.

This is no mere flight of fancy: Garfield is a killer. In the great badger state of Wisconsin, farm cats are estimated to kill between 7 and 100 million birds annually. Each of Great Britain's 6 to 8 million cats murder seven to eight birds a year, more for feral rural toms, less for high-rise fat cats whose claws rarely touch ground, but a rough total of about 50 million birds, according to the British Trust for Ornithology.

And how many similarly disposed little leopards pad the whole of the United States? Some 63.8 million "owned cats," according to the Pet Food Institute in Washington, DC, and God knows how many more in the wild. So you don't have to be John James Audubon with an abacus to realize we are talking a very unnatural predator to prey relationship here, perhaps a cat epidemic, and, for sure, a whole lot of eviscerated robins.

University of Wisconsin researchers actually put radio collars on 32 cats, numbered another 90, and sent written questionnaires to several thousand rural homes: "Dear Respondent: Is Mittens with her kittens? Or is she outside, ripping the lungs from a lark?"

Should cats be banned? Belled? "Emotionally delisted" as a species and shot like coyotes? Or perhaps Tom and Tabitha need only be confined to quarters, placed under stringent curfew from, say, 8 PM to 9 AM, as are all cats in Victoria, Australia, a city that discovered its half million cats put away 12 million small animals each year, including 76 bird species, 67 of which were native and in danger of extinction. Cat owners who violate the curfew must pay $100—more than it would cost to neuter and declaw.

But neutering, while it certainly helps to limit successive generations, does nothing to tone down the hunting instinct, and even removing a cat's claws—ouch!—does not dent their ability to pounce, crush, and snap necks (to the extent that birds have necks). A cat's sharp, all-canine teeth could also be extracted, but who would be so cruel, except, perhaps, a British vegetarian? Already, some vegetarians are feeding their cats a meatless kibble in the mistaken hope that cats will calm down and adapt to their owners' spiritual beliefs. But cats, be they lions, leopards, or tortoiseshells, have not changed their basic menu of meat, milk, and meat since the first lynxlike Ur-cat of the Miocene. Cats are not bears. They do not like strawberries. If you give your cat vegetarian food rather than meat protein, you are only condemning nearby birds to certain death from a genetically starved predator.

To take the pressure off the local bird population, several halfway measures are recommended. Hang bird feeders away from bushes and cover. Use Catwatch, a commercial sonic movement detector that sweeps the birdy area with a high-frequency noise that greatly pisses off cats. Cover ground bird nests with wire mesh small enough to keep cats out yet large enough to allow mother and father bird back in. Less work and more fun: Mount freezer bags full of water by the back door to bomb visiting felines or, if you prefer, high-pressure water pistols. Owning one cat is better than none, because your pet will quickly establish territory and discourage encroachers.

Opinion is divided as to belling. "It's a daft bird that can't fly off when a belled cat lunges the last few feet," says C. J. Mead, who conducted the British studies. Counters Dr. John S. Coleman, at the University of Wisconsin, "Cats, especially when seriously stalking, walk in such a way that the bell doesn't ring until the final pounce. The bell is the last thing that bird will ever hear."

Cats are not the only reason some 70% of the world's birds are in decline, including some 1000 species that may soon go extinct. Loss of habitat, pesticides (DDT, banned in the United States and Europe, is widely used elsewhere), and oil spills (the *Exxon Valdez* alone killed some 300,000 sea birds)— all take their toll. The increasingly sanitary nature of modern agriculture removes bugs and worms and introduces nonnative plants, creating a curiously silent spring in which plenty of adult birds sing and hop about while their fledglings starve in the midst of greenness.

Overhunting, too, has discouraged the life out of some birds—passenger pigeons, for instance, or the 3 million neotropical migrants shot over the small island of Malta annually. The Italians eat 50 million songbirds each year. One Italian game warden recently busted a restaurant with 1400 plucked robins in the kitchen. Those Europeans will eat anything! Here's how they like their finches: blackened, grilled, and plucked but not gutted, deboned, debeaked, or beheaded. The finch is popped into the mouth whole, rather like a cat would dine. Crunch. *Buon appetito!*

I happen to enjoy wing-shooting pheasants myself, also quail, if I am able to hit them, and I have, on a couple of trouting trips when the trout were not cooperating, bashed in the heads of curious sage hens with the hand net, so hold the e-mail. But is it fair to call Europeans barbarous omnivores just because they eat birds that sing? After all, elk bugle.

The bottom line is availability. Are we about down to the last auk? Or are there so many of a species, like cats (also deer, magpies, and us), that, unregulated, they are eating other creatures out of habitat and home? Cats, after all, are subsidized by free food handouts, just as deer numbers are kept high by wiping out wolves.

We all have our prejudices, or we would not be human. I happen to like birds and cats both. Our cat is a small tabby named Onca, which means jaguar in Brazilian Portuguese. We got her to rid the house of marauding voles, which she did in one day and a night. Then she went out in the yard and rammed her fist into the bluebird boxes. Then she got herself a boyfriend, a snow-white biker of a tom, whose tail had been pinched off somehow and who looked as if he slept in an abandoned vat at the Black Dog Brewery. When he comes a-courting, you want to leave the garage armed with a stick, though it's not hard to tell if he's under the car, because he makes it sound as if the engine is already on.

I would never eat a cat, though, unless paid to, as I once was, by a San Francisco newspaper, when I was traveling through Gwangchou, southern China, and I went to a restaurant where snake was also served. The dish I had was called Dragon-Phoenix-Tiger (snake-chicken-cat) Soup, but I am not sure it was the best game restaurant in Asia. All the flavors kind of ran together, and it tasted pretty much like finch.

Blowing Away the
Media/TV Hunting

It is a soft spring day in Montana's Hyalite Canyon. The hill is spaced with stumps and Douglas fir. We walk slowly along a path at the 6000-foot level. Below, the rasp of the creek across granite masks the sounds of our breathing. Suddenly, from behind a stand of aspen, there is the glint of a Sony. Strobel levels his .20 gauge and fires but, incredibly, the spray of bird shot only *pings* off the screen. Could the console charge? I drop to one knee and let loose with my .45. There is the satisfying *thunk* of bullet against cathode. Our quarry implodes in a flash of yellow, orange, and blue and spins down the slope, end over end, antenna chasing power cord, until it comes to rest against a lichen-covered boulder at our feet.

"You won't hear any more *Love Boat* reruns in *these* woods," says Strobel.

He's right. It's been a good day's hunting: two Sonys, a Mitsubishi, and a two-point Sylvania. (All TVs tend to be two-pointers, unless rigged for cable, in which case they are considered does and can only be taken in special hunts.) We lay out the gutted televisions in the snow for a trophy shot.

In Montana, you see, we don't watch TVs. We shoot them. We don't have a few beers and catch the game. We have no beers and blow the game away.

Electronic rights activists may squawk, but TV hunting is as American as bait-fishing. Primal recreation.

Typically, a TV hunt such as the one Strobel and I arranged is a stocked, or "New York," hunt, the prey arrayed on separate stumps after being scrounged from rec room and garage or purchased at local pawn and thrift shops. The truly committed pack in generators so that the targets glow blue in the bushes. The element of cultural revenge is stronger in a live TV hunt, since you really get to implode Ted Koppel, Rush Limbaugh, Barney, or the ever-erroneous weatherperson (take your choice).

Aldous Huxley, the author of *Brave New World*, once wrote: "A society most of whose members spend a great part of their time, not on the spot, not here and now and in the calculable future, but somewhere else, in the irrelevant other worlds of sports and soap opera, of mythology and metaphysical fantasy, will find it hard to resist the encroachment of those who would manipulate and control it."

True. And when Huxley referred to "sports," I don't think he meant TV hunting, since televisions were not widespread in his time, nor, obviously, is the hunting of them a be-fatted spectator sport, which is what he loathed. Though Huxley, as a meek British person, could not come right out and say it, I am sure he would have agreed: TV hunting is the one thing that will save Western civilization from itself.

Undeniably, TV hunting is one of the last freedoms left. There are no government regulations (yet). No bag limits. The hunting of televisions is one of those spontaneous American expressions that surface in the darkest hours, when the *McLaughlin Report* cannot be switched off quickly enough. Something large is afoot here. We need interactive shopping channels about as much as geese need cheeseburgers. There is some brutality connected with TV hunting, admittedly, but there is much violence on television, too.

TV hunting, as a socially redeeming sport, got its start July 4, 1982, on Montana's Sindelar Ranch, when wealthy rancher Brian Sindelar left a cryptic message on his nephew Will McLaughlin's answering machine: "I have a renegade television on my property. I want you boys to come out and help me."

Will, then 15, brought his Winchester 30.06 lever action. Will's high school buddy, Dave Strobel, who years later would be my TV guide for the Hyalite hunt, brought along his grandfather's single-shot 20 gauge. At the ranch they found a trail of cut TV plugs and half-buried bits of copper wire. Sindelar, like most TV hunters, had his rules. If he judged that the set could "see" or "smell" the boys before they saw or smelled it, he rehid the TV. The boys were told to shoot fast, before the channels changed. At the end of the hunt, Sindelar tagged the antennas and Will and Dave hauled the carcasses to the dump. Thus was a sport born.

TV hunting is not for everybody, of course, not even for every decent person with a gun, but if it is for you, there are some things you should know. The white powder that puffs out when bullet bites screen can be quite poisonous, like the powder in fluorescent lights. Let the dust settle before checking your kill. There is also some danger of being hit by shrapnel, especially at close range.

Decoys do not make sense in TV hunting. Practicing, though possible, is not practical, either. You can throw the sets up like skeet, but it's a mess on the ground, like using live pigeons. The ecologically correct—and what hunter these days is not?—spreads canvas or a plastic tarp under the televisions.

Let us beware of image, because television hunting is a sport for our times. Never mind that the media have been careful to ignore the growing phenomenon, so far—and naturally enough. What

Santa Monica producer wishes to admit that True Americans live to drill her creations with double O buckshot? The media in this country may be reviled, but they are not stupid.

In fact, TV hunting could easily be co-opted. I can imagine one of those video *verité* shows following hunters into the local Powder Horn, asking which ammo is best for the new flat screens. The tumble of tube down ravine is mighty visual stuff, and it cannot be long before Geraldo films "Men Who Hunt TVs." Others will follow: "2020 with a 30.30." Nintendo will come out with its most popular game: "TV Hunt!"

But if the sport catches on, as I believe it must, Americans will return to their homes purged after a day of stalking the wild Sylvania. A calm will settle into our living rooms. Parents will once again talk with their children, and they will be heard, and the children will smile. Respect will be interactive and mutual. Lovers will make love without video aids, seeing the real person underneath or above them. The musically inclined will pluck acoustic instruments. They will not channel surf. Their weapons will be warm in locked cabinets, and their minds free.

In America, it is tough to beat the media, but, if you're a good shot, it is still possible to cream them.

Exercise your rights.

Tavern Animals

There is a hole of a bar in Tonopah, Nevada, a place as far from the meaning of "sport" as good is from evil (unless you accept the jack-lighting of Gila monsters as the way it should be) where a live rattlesnake is kept sequestered in a large pickle jar.

The deal with the snake is that you put your hand on the outside of the jar. In your other hand you hold up a $5 bill. You must keep your eyes open. The snake's cage is lined with $5 bills from earlier braggarts who were unable to keep their palms against the glass when the snake struck, which is just about immediately. In fact, to date, no one has ever not flinched.

Further north and to the east of Tonopah, at the Stockman in Fairview, Montana, swims a different sort of tavern animal. Unlike the rattler of Tonopah, which, of course, does not swim, this creature has a name: Fat Boy. I first encountered Fat Boy, the celebrated Thai puffer fish of Richland County, while we ourselves were celebrating, bourbon and champagne for the adults, sarsaparillas and chili for the kids. We had just finished floating and fishing our way down the entire length of the Yellowstone to the Missouri confluence. The barmaid (they still have barmaids in eastern Montana) asked if we might want "to buy one for Fat Boy, also."

"What's Fat Boy drink?" I asked.

"Well, I suppose what he drinks is water, but what you buy for him is a goldfish."

Never was a quarter more dramatically spent. The barmaid produced a little net, scooped up a goldfish from a plastic bag under the bar, and plopped it into Fat Boy's tank. The wedge-shaped puffer lunged with an alacrity surprising in one so corpulent, sucking the goldfish into his maw without chewing, and burped out a satisfied little bubble into a hank of aquarium grass afterward.

Three-hundred-fifty-four miles south of Fat Boy's tank at the Stockman, and somewhat upriver, there is, or at least there used to be, a cat who drank bourbon. This was at the Grizzly Bar (now the Grizzly Bar & Grill) in Roscoe. You'd be on a hunting trip around the foot of the Beartooths, and late in the afternoon, you'd want to wet your whistle in preparation for dinner. The owner of the Grizzly would invite you to buy a bourbon for The Cat.

"Cats don't drink bourbon," you'd reply, but too late. The owner was already slapping a trick jigger glass on the bar and a somewhat inebriated tabby was wobbling toward you. Owner would pour some brown liquid into the glass, also inviting you to test it in your own glass. Tabby'd be lapping hers up like cream. It turned out that the drink really was bourbon, but, of course, the rim of the cat's glass had been smeared with tuna oil, and the cat well-trained. In a few months, or a year, that cat succumbed to some sort of kitty cirrhosis of the liver and was replaced by a new recruit.

Nobody protested in the old days, sadly. It's hard to believe that only a few centuries before, "Cat Organs" would be paraded down the streets of medieval towns, driven by a chained bear wearing a muzzle, and from time to time the poor bear would yank a cat's tail, producing an awful organlike yowl. We are more enlightened now. We have satellite dishes the size of small pizzas, and nobody would laugh if politicians, sandwiched into Wurlitzer organs, were bitten at musical intervals by mako sharks riding—

But this is a serious subject. For purposes of obfuscation and brevity, tavern animals can be divided into two categories: the Stuffed and the Still Biting. We already know about the still biting and, besides, the dead, as is often true in life, hold out more mystery.

Why, for instance, do jackalopes, those rabbitty deer creatures you see mounted everywhere above the cash registers of taverns in the Mountain West, feed only by the light of a full moon? And why do beazles, or fur-bearing trout, avoid hot springs unless an angler bumps snow worms across the bottom? Why, for that matter, do the mahogany monkeys of the Middle Fork stand so perfectly still in the crooks of trees at streamside that they rarely make it to bars at all?

In science, there is a simple explanation for most all phenomena. Jackalopes, or Warrior Rabbits, feed under a full moon because full moon nights are generally clearer and the animals' voices carry better. If pursued, and jackalopes are still hunted for their meat in places like Chugwater, Wyoming, they can shout, "He's there, in that clump of mesquite!" or, "Watch out behind you!"

Live jackalopes have a command of English rare in this day and age and can even throw their voices. Nobody knows how they do it. What is known is that their milk is already homogenized, from all the jumping, and that women, at least Wyoming women, should not drink it. (It is also believed, but harder to prove, that jackalopes copulate only during lightning flashes.)

The origin of the fur-bearing trout is even more interesting. Fur-bearing trout were once regular trout, but as the Elk Mountain (Colorado) *Pilot* reported, February 23, 1939, a Kentucky man, journeying to the gold camp at Leadville, fell off his mule while crossing the Arkansas and broke two jugs of hair tonic on a rock. The Kentucky man was headed for Leadville because he was a Republican and wanted to avoid the taxes then levied on small businessmen in Kentucky, and because many of the miners in Leadville were bald, for reasons that had nothing to do with tavern animals, though in the interests of literature, I must quote the *Pilot* verbatim as to why:

> During the winter of 1877 and 1878, meat was supplied to the miners in the form of venison by professional game hunters. They ate so much venison and fried potatoes that the venison tallow became caked in the roofs of their mouths to the extent that they were unable to taste their coffee and other beverages. This was indeed distressing and often they eliminated this handicap by wiring a bundle of pitch splinters on top of their heads and setting fire to it. The result was that the tallow was melted and they again had the sense of taste, but the net result was that 97% of the miners in that camp became baldheaded.

After the accident with the hair tonic, the trout in the river began to sprout fur, which gave them a genetic advantage in those cold waters. They began to flourish.

Not long after that, reported the *Pilot,* "the trout fishermen of the vicinity changed their methods. Instead of the usual rod and reel, they would go down to the creek on Saturday afternoon, stick a red, white, and blue pole in the bank, put on a white coat, wave a copy of the *Police Gazette* in one hand, and brandish a scissors in the other, and yell, 'Next!'"

This practice continued, explained the newspaper, "until mine tailings from the mills riled the water so that the trout could no longer see the barber poles."

I suppose there are some who would say we hang walrus penises and white rabbits with deer antlers above our heads in taverns because we just want to enjoy a good laugh in a comfortable, smoke-filled setting, crush beer cans against our foreheads, and dream of better days, after having pulled the hook out of the chukar's mouth and missing the brown. And this makes sense.

Why else would the unstuffed French anthropologist Claude Lévi-Strauss, after a morel foray outside Miles City, Montana, begin an essay for a learned taxidermic journal: "There is a heaven and there is a God, and there are my wife's breasts—"

Possibly, because there are people who will attempt any trick in order to exit a piece of writing.

Even so, I believe it *was* Lévi-Strauss, before he formed the late 1980s disco-thrash band The Fine Young Cannibals and wrote the hit, "The Raw & The Cooked," who first advanced the theory that we hang walrus penises and white rabbits with deer antlers sprouting from their heads upon our barroom walls because we feel we must sooth the spirits of the Rabbit People and the Walrus People for having so recently clubbed and shot them to death. In other words, tavern animals represent an appeasement, in fur and feathers.

This is silly, of course, and silliness should have no place among serious hunters and fishers. No wonder the French have so few fur-bearing trout left in their streams, and even fewer elk.

Trolling the Tropics

There comes a point in any man's life when he is in need of spiritual uplift. This point comes to me seasonally, at the sight of the first hard autumn rain. Sometimes I can last till first snow.

Then it is time to abandon San Francisco or southwestern Montana, where I now live, since the fishing's better, and force myself (with family) to endure the confinements of jet travel to Kona, Rio de Janeiro, perhaps central Africa, which these days is an underrated tropical destination. This winter I found myself rappelling down the Zambezi, which is just like the Sacramento, really, only with more crocodiles.

In the tropical slide, the leaving is as important as the getting there. The worse the weather upon takeoff, the more pleasant that first margarita at Huggo's, over the waves in Kona on the Big Island of Hawaii; the first *caipirinha* at Alberico's, across from the beach in Ipanema; the first Zambezi Slammer on the rim of a gorge for a river where some of the standing waves are big enough to surf 16-foot Avon Expedition rafts backward.

There is something about drinking a Slammer in a bathing suit while watching a family of warthogs disport themselves on the lip of Victoria Falls that is superior to popping a Schmidts in a Minneapolis blizzard.

For me, arriving in the tropics each year is like starting life over, the eternal spring, "Golden Bough" stuff, only with fewer mythopoeic trappings and, of course, local custom permitting, less clothing.

As the moon rises insouciantly over the palms at Rio's Carnival Sambadrome and the first wave of

2000 *sambistas* comes twirling between the grandstands, insouciant sweat gliding down insouciant nipples, it is time for those of my pale tribe to sigh and say, once more: "Get thee behind me, Devil!"

Changes in latitude. Changes in attitude.

And I am not alone.

Twain, Stevenson, Melville, Lawrence, Darwin in the Galapagos, Hemingway in Key West, Somerset Maugham in Pago Pago, Gaugin in Papeete, Bukowski in San Pedro (cold is relative), Waugh in Guyana, John Huston in Africa, Tennessee Williams, also in Key West. A long list of venerables who, confined to a less tropical island such as Manhattan or England, would only have churned out back-biting prose and wasted their winters going to lunch.

To be sure, a guy list. The tropics seem to work the other way for women. Women want to get the hell out of the languor. Think of Doris Lessing leaving Zimbabwe without ever having, so far as we know, sport-rafted the Zambezi, or Germane Greer escaping the local man pool (and her mother) in Australia for the imagined bright lights of London and New York.

Men go in search of the primitive. Women like cats. Thank God, that is ending. Increasingly, women are returning to the rainforests in search of those most primitive of men, the apes. Jane Goodall's chimpanzees, Birute Galdikas's orangutans, Diane Fossey's mountain gorillas. These women are a new breed, wilder than the stymied Greers and Lessings, rowdier in real life than the Hollywood movies made about them; in fact, more like the Hemingways, Hustons, and Gaugins, set loose by life in the jungles.

The shy Judeo-Christian Coalition side of some

of us is somehow unhinged by the languid slide into warm weather. At swim inside an unconscious not awakened by snowplows, we can more easily access our churning creative cores. We work better down under.

The tropics keep the momentum going, and momentum is everything, in writing, in life, in travel. Fertile minds turn to salt under conditions of inclement weather, the dreary floods of this last winter in northern California, for instance.

Tropical sliders may look hardy in a wet suit, but they grow torpid and bleary-eyed without sun. The biorhythmic sadness caused by late 8 AM dawns is sloughed off on islands and archipelagos so close to the equator that sunlight stays the same year round and there are no time changes. Also, so long as your tropics lie to the west, your medulla oblongata will be fooled into waking you earlier. In Kona, I often leave the house as the sun bolts through the saddle in the volcano, which puts me in the lagoon at Kahaluu, 1000 feet down the mountain, at about 5:30, just as the *humuhumunukunuku apuai'a* fish go swimming by and the turtles take a last graze on the algae before flippering for deep water. This is the way to wake up, goggle-eyed inside a prescription face mask—not jogging in a raincoat.

Once behind the laptop, there are fewer interruptions. Nobody from New York will call you in Hawaii. It is a 6-hour time difference, costs too much, and they have no idea where the Pacific is, anyway.

"If the house [in Connecticut] would only burn down," Mark Twain wrote Charles Warren Stoddard in Hawaii in 1881, "we would pack up the cubs and fly to the isles of the blest, and shut ourselves up in the healing solitudes of Haleakala and get a good rest; for the mails do not intrude there, nor yet the telephone and the telegraph."

To work well in Hawaii, you must be careful to be off the beach between 9 and 3. Otherwise, you will sit before the screen alert and lively as a plantain. Air conditioning is necessary. Cold beer is necessary.

I know an IBM inventor who keeps a dry, hot, airy beach house on Kealakekua Bay with one cold room, his office. It costs him more to run that frosty appliance than to power the rest of the house, but it pays for everything else, since it allows him to think.

I like tropical music, the lick-samba and guava jelly of Bob Marley, the unphasable lilt of bossa nova, the savannah rhythm of Thomas Mapfume and the Africans who started it all. I like the colors. The flowers wake me up—jacaranda, bougainvillae, flamboyant shameless-marias. Even the names cheer me.

So, too, the easy sensuality, especially the separation of sex from violence. In America, sex and violence are married. It is our British heritage: We can't feel love without pain. But nobody talks about rape or pornography in Brazil or Polynesia, while violence is mostly reserved for the weather, for the hurricanes, and for mundane economic matters such as crime and revolution. (Love, in the tropics, as everywhere, is a rare commodity.)

Changes in attitude, changes in latitude.

I like the latitude shown toward family and children. For all the recent bombast about family values in America from major politicians like Newt, Bill, and Bill Bennett—each one from a broken and violent home, naturally—America just doesn't like kids anymore, at least the way they do in Brazil, Hawaii, and the South Seas. People are busy to the point of meanness in the United States, ambitious to the point of cruelty, so far as children are concerned.

If, in the aftermath of a bank robbery in Rio de Janeiro, a small child should run between police and escaping criminals, the bank robbers would most likely tuck pistols in belts and carry the toddler back to police lines. Then the shooting would begin again. In America, the poor kid would be used as a shield, probably, I suppose, by the robbers.

Unfortunately, by age 12 in Brazil, you are no longer considered to be a kid.

The tropics are not for everyone. Bliss can be a guilty burden. *The Mosquito Coast* was written for these folks. As fine a book and movie as it is, this tragedy of going too far is a simple cautionary tale. "Why, oh, why, oh/Did I ever leave Ohio/When life was so cozy at home?"—as the old song goes. *The Mosquito Coast* tells people to stay in the good ole USA and put away tropical fantasies, or else.

Others like the tropics too much ever to return home. Stevenson wrote, "Few men who come to the islands leave them; they grow grey where they alighted; the palm shades and the trade-wind fans them till they die . . . "

Staying too long presents its own problems. You could go *tropo,* an Australian turn of phrase defined as *a confused and often demented state of mind.*

So, there are a few problems with the tropics: madness, fever, tiger sharks, tigers, crime, rot.

Life is hard anywhere, but back home it is hard and cold.

Bugz

"Musquetoes troublesome," Meriwether Lewis,
May 23, 1805
"Musquetors troublesome," William Clark,
May 23, 1805
"Musquetors verry troublesom," Clark,
July 2, 1805
"Musquetos troublesome as usual," Lewis,
July 8, 1805
"Musquitors verry troublesom," Clark,
July 20, 1805
"Musquetoes uncommonly large and reather
troublesome," Lewis, July 29, 1806
"Musquetoes extreemly troublesome," Lewis,
July 12, 1806
"Musquetors excessively troublesom," Clark,
August 2, 1806
"Musquitors excessively tormenting," Clark,
September 7, 1806

There are 700,000 different kinds of known insects, 2700 species of mosquitoes, 90,000 flies, 30,000 ticks (actually eight-legged fellows related to spiders), 1800 fleas, 3500 cockroaches, and one really loathsome kind of bedbug. For each one of us, there are 200 million of them, which sifts out to about 300 pounds of bugs per person. The biomass of the ants alone weighs more than all humans put together. It gives pause.

Insects eat our zucchini. They poke holes in our squash. They discomfort us mightily at stream side.

And it only gets worse.

"Since the beginning of recorded history insects have caused the death by disease of more people than all the wars, earthquakes, hurricanes, floods, droughts and fires combined. To this immense toll of human life," reads a report for the American Museum of Natural History, "can be added incalculable economic losses caused by insects attacking food and textile crops, forests, buildings, furniture and much else."

I don't know about the furniture, but I think this might be too strong an indictment of our tiny friends, the joint-footed Arthropoda. If it weren't for caddis flies, also mayflies and maybe black gnats, trout would starve, along with a goodly number of stream-running bass and walleyes.

Things balance out. It's important to keep your perspective, though the bloodsuckers can easily give you Lyme disease, make you crazy as a bedbug, drive you antsy, or—

Everybody has a scorpion in the ear story, a tale of wasps inside the tent. I remember a time in my youth (an extended and larvaelike period, looking back on it) when I became fresh meat for a large herd of *musquetors* along the shores of Fossil Lake, in the Beartooth Wilderness of Montana and northern Wyoming, where I happened to be whiling away a weekend prospecting for albino golden trout.

I was off the trail, above the tree line. There were billowing clouds of them, the *muskitors*, and since it was June, they had me to themselves. It was too late for elk and moose, too early for the more inviting German backpackers, who, in my experience, wear little else but sunscreen and shards of leiderhosen.

My feelings were described perfectly by Roger W. Crosskey, entomologist with the British Museum: "The experience of being continually bitten, unable to step outside without soon oozing blood from countless bites, is a demoralizer with few equals." This from Crosskey's remarkable treatise, *The Natural History of Blackflies.*

But these brutes were bigger than blackflies. "Two of them could whip a dog," as Mark Twain said of some "lawless insects" down South. "Four of them could hold a man down; and except help come, they would kill him—butcher him."

I had no tent, back in Montana, no prophylaxis, save a clear plastic raincoat I'd picked up at the Army Navy Store in Billings for, in those days, about $4.95. I threw it over my T-shirt and jeans and zipped it up. It was the pants-suit kind, and it did the trick. Then I began to sweat. Then, as my core temperature slowly rose and the mozzies whined and whinnied outside my vinyl exoskeleton, I grew mad as a bedbug. Mine was becoming a Kafkaesque camping experience. I thought I might be undergoing some terrible metamorphosis—like a caribou. Already, extreme bedevilment was causing me to mix metaphors.

As you know, it is not unknown for caribou, in Canada, to sometimes charge into the nearest lake or river, even if that means drowning, should squadrons of blackflies descend. If there is an insect hell on earth, it is probably Canada, the whole country.

"The little [blackflies] force their way into any crevice," complained early Colossus-to-the-North explorers Louis Agassiz and Henry Walter Bates, near Lake Superior; "On the other hand they are easily killed, as they stick to their prey like bulldogs."

Personally, in fly season, I am afraid to venture north of the Milk River, and it has nothing to do with Margaret Atwood, Margaret Trudeau, or backbacon.

They are a formidable enemy, the crinkly foot Arthropoda. At Fossil Lake, I lit a smudge stick from a moss-covered spruce branch and ceded the area to superior forces.

"Life on this planet can get along well without people," asserts one author who has dedicated his life to this sort of thing, "but it cannot in its present form do without insects. Without them we would die."

There would be no flowers without insects. The two evolved together. No apple trees or cactus, either. Can't live with them, can't live without them. Which brings us to the sex life of the mantids, at last.

When a male praying mantis jumps on a receptive female praying mantis, and they have only just begun to mate, the female turns over her shoulder and bites off the male's head, which she then proceeds to eat. Interestingly, the male, though now headless, does not draw back from his business. Once in a great while he does, out of lassitude or gravity, but if so, another male flies aboard. She bites his head off, too. That's how it's done in the mantid world, and bug scientists even believe the male's decapitation is the dramatic signal that causes him to release his sperm, or, since his head has just been chewed and swallowed, I believe it might be more accurate to say, *causes his sperm to be released.*

At any rate, it does not have to be this way, and it is not for most insects. Certainly, not for the bedbug, a true bug, of the homoptera, or True Bugs.

Since lady bedbugs have no genital opening (yes, I know this is a family publication, but we are talking about creepy-crawlies) he ups and pokes a hole between her fifth and six abdominal segments. This probably hurts a lot, but the female bedbug is equipped with something called an organ of Berlese, which functions, claims entomologist May R. Berenbaum,

> to prevent the male's organ from doing permanent physical injury to her internal anatomy. The male bedbug then pumps in an enormous quantity of sperm, which swim into the bloodstream and eventually find the reproductive organs of the female. After the male withdraws his organ, the wound he created eventually closes and heals over, leaving a scar. The whole process is called, appropriately, traumatic insemination.

Clearly, it is a dull business, studying bugs for a living.

Modern chemicals have all but eliminated the grosser behaviors of the bedbug, along with the bedbugs themselves, most of them. Count yourself lucky this spring that you only have to shoo away the flies, squeeze off the sand fleas, and apply hot match heads to the tick butts sequestered in your secret places. Be thankful that bedbugs don't swarm.

Also, don't whine. The frequency of human whining only attracts certain beetles, anyway, like wasps to cologne.

It could be worse. In the late Carboniferous Period, dragonflies were 3 feet long, and primitive *musquetoes* stretched 8 inches, thoraxes thick as axe handles, with stingers like sailing needles. There was a lot more oxygen then.

And don't try to eat them. You already are. I like shrimp, lobster, and crab—and these are the insects of the sea. Ask any biologist.

Strive to be strong, this bug season, even as you

are pierced and sucked, bored and drilled. We are Americans, and we must act like Americans, not like Canadians or quitter French persons.

Remember, if Napoleon's brother-in-law, General Charles Leclerc, had not turned tail in his vainglorious attempt to conquer Haiti and the fledgling United States after only 29,000 of the 33,000 men he set sail from Paris with had died of yellow fever, we might all be grilling truffles on hot plates. Lewis and Clark would never have made it up the Yellowstone, with all the sauger, sturgeon, pike, paddlefish, and cutthroat trout this implies, since there would have been no Louisiana Purchase. The Yellow Stone would have stayed *La Roche Jahne.* You could say the "*troublesom musquetor*" was the bug that won the West.

Insects cannot be all bad.

Dinosaur Season

Don't ask me how you got there, perhaps in a pink Cadillac, but you are in Mongolia, dinosaur hunting. It might just as well be Montana. They looked a lot alike 90 million years ago.

Naturally, you're a bit disoriented, stalking through a prehistoric palm forest that seems strangely denuded. There is little undergrowth, a few dogwoods and berry bushes, but grass has not yet evolved. Some furry little creatures are running away from you. They look like skinny badgers with bad teeth. These are your people: the mammals. But why do they look so terrified? Then you understand their problem. Over the volcanic ridge something very large bellows. The genetic memory deep within your hindbrain stirs like a blender. Mixed with the bellowing rises a keening scream. You drop to your knees.

Then you remember: Hey, I'm an American. I'm armed. It's my right to hunt dinosaurs. This is, after all, what I'm doing here in the late Cretaceous. Still, it's best to be cautious. You sling your weapon onto your back and slither to the edge of the overlook.

Tales of the Xenozoic! Down in the sand dunes by the inland sea, a velociraptor is doing battle with a protoceratops. That is, a lightly built meat-eater— two-legged and upright with a long flat snout, about the size of a small mountain lion—is swinging its foot claw at a 3-ton herbivorous dinosaur as armor-plated as a troop carrier.

The velociraptor's claw startles you. A hundred yards below you, it glints with dinosaur blood, and it is about 6 inches long. The velociraptor stands first on one leg than on the other, slashing like a fighting cock, or an ostrich, which can disembowel an African lion with its considerably smaller spur.

For its part, the ceratopsian moves like a sumo wrestler. It wants to butt. If it can gather momentum against the swifter velociraptor, it will crush it like an orange against a steel wall.

The breeze shifts, and you shift quickly with it, breaking twigs and scuffling frond leaves. You know you must stay upwind. What you are hunting has the visual acuity of an eagle and can see in color, unlike an elk or a cat. Yet it has the ferocity and moves of a mountain lion and the sense of smell—and the sociability—of a wolf. It may well have traveled in packs. We don't know. But watch your back. The one advantage you have over the carnosaurs is hearing, especially the larger members, like *Tyrannosaurus rex*. They might not be able to hear high-frequency sounds like twigs breaking.

So you're a little nervous, even if the *velo* down there is only as smart as a smart turkey. That's smart enough, and it is his world. Something else bothers you, suddenly. You've masked your scent—this is the only way to stalk a dinosaur, since its sense of smell is worlds better than ours and, for that matter, a deer's—but since you decided before you went into this that you wanted to taste the flesh of a ceratopsian, the black rhino of the Cretaceous, you took care to roll in the first dry fibrous dung you found. Now, to a carnivore such as the velociraptor or *T. rex*, you smell exactly like—prey.

Still, you're good. You've got angle, up on the ridge. The *velo* can hit 40 miles/hour at magpie stride, but he's below and doesn't see you. You take aim on the bucking and weaving protoceratops. This is fair chase, so far, and you kill only what you intend to eat. You're in this all the way, for barbecue.

According to what you've read, you're not to go for a head shot. The ceratopsians had very small brains protected by thick head plates, so it's got to be a heart shot. In contrast to mammals, their hearts were huge. You're now trying to position yourself for a three-quarter frontal, because in most four-legged dinosaurs, the shoulder blade wrapped around the cardiac chamber. This is for a clean kill, and even in this prehistoric age, one should strive to be politically correct.

The paleontologists you had talked to at the University of California, and at Yale, had counseled (off the record) that a medium bore, high-velocity rifle would be adequate. Bob Bakker, the curator at the Tate Museum in Wyoming and a consultant to the movie *Jurassic Park,* had laughed, "Will you be hunting with a high-powered rifle and infrared scope, or backpack and Birkenstocks?" The first time you called Bakker, you had reached his answering machine: "Hello, this is Guido, the komodo dragon. Sorry, I can't come to the phone right now because I'm eating a tourist."

So, Bakker had seemed to be a likely helpmate, even if he had urged you only to arm yourself with a video camera: "High speed, good zoom, keep your head *down* ! "

Forget that.

Bakker is the wild philosopher among paleontologists. He pushed early and hard for the theory, increasingly accepted, that many dinosaurs were warm-blooded, more like birds than reptiles. But, right now, Bob Bakker is conveniently back in Casper, Wyoming, and you, conveniently or not, are squeezing off your first shot from the ridge.

It misses.

The velociraptor jabbed. The protoceratops

shifted. Your shot pinged off the head plate like a .22 shot off a Serbian tank.

You curse Bakker. "I wouldn't think you should need anything so heavy as the rifles the early African explorers used on elephants," he had said.

Forget elephants. They haven't evolved yet, either. The dinosaurs stare up at your lookout. They pause and sniff, like wolf and moose. Tingles trip along your spine, and then an incredible thing happens. They turn back on each other. The protoceratops rams. The velociraptor leaps and stabs, and its claw pierces the plant-eater's heart. At the same time, the battering ram of the 'ceratops creams the snouty bird head of the 'raptor.

They're both dead. It is as if a bull elk crushed the head of a grizzly at the same time as the grizzly ripped out the elk's vitals. In 1971, a fossil of just such a battle was found in Mongolia, a velociraptor's foot-claw embedded in the chest cavity of a protoceratops, both very ancient history.

You are stunned. But you are also hungry.

You creep down the hill, a bit warily. Perhaps you should have gone fishing. The sea below churns with alligator gar and paddlefish. You could have packed a crossbow, maybe a folding kayak. Of course, your paleontologist friends had mentioned the fast-swimming lizards called plesiosaurs with heads 10 feet long (not counting neck), bodies 20 to 60 feet long, and flippers like those of giant paddling penguins. They could out-swim one of our great whites, the progenitors of which there were already too many, plying the waves of the Cretaceous. These fellows were a bit bigger than the great white sharks we have today, 30-plus feet and counting. The fossil record is not reassuring. In the late Cretaceous, you would probably want to cast from shore.

You're down on the valley floor now.

Dinner time, but Jesus (also not yet evolved) what does a dinosaur taste like? Being more related to birds than reptiles, dinosaurs would not taste like alligator tail. They would taste more like . . . chicken.

Wild fowl taste like what they have been eating, the way antelope taste like sage. The big brontosaur ate conifers, pine needles. Perhaps their flesh would have had an interesting aromatic flavor.

Indeed. Well, this thought does not put you less on edge as you carve off a protoceratops steak. You insert your knife into the slash made by the velociraptor, since the hide of the herbivore is even thicker than a rhino's would be.

As you carve, you note how still the tidal plain has become. But you don't think about that for long. You are annoyed at how difficult it is to start a fire without grass or hardwood. Any pines are back up on the ridge. You should have brought a backpacker's stove, you think, or maybe you should try dino sashimi . . .

The ground is shaking. You drop the knife.

It is a real *T. rex*, 20 feet tall, 40 feet long, a tail as massive as two loaded canoes. Your thoughts come in gulps now. *What if I see a Tyrannosaurus?* And Bakker had replied, "A full grown *Tyrannosaurus rex* would have weighed some 7000 pounds. We would be to a *Tyrannosaurus* as mice are to a lion, neither worth eating nor worth chasing." *Good, good, but what if I do see one?* "In *Jurassic Park*, the people escape the *Tyrannosaurus* by standing still. That is absurd. The animal had an acute sense of smell. It was probably a rather smart creature, too." *Did it eat carrion or live food?* "My personal view is that it was omnivorous." *Could you outrun it?* "Hard to say. If you had nowhere to go, I suppose you might be done for. But then, unless it was a female and she had babies with her, not to worry."

Behind her tail, you see the cubs.

Dinner Bell Grizzlies

These bears, being so hard to die, rather intimidate us all. I must confess that I do not like the gentlemen and had rather fight two Indians than one bear. There is no other chance to conquer them by a single shot but by shooting them through the brains . . .
—Meriwether Lewis, along the Yellowstone, May 11, 1805

Nothing freezes the human hindbrain quicker than the sight of a grizzly, close-up, except for sharks and polar bears, both of which are rare in northeastern Wyoming.

In the old days in Wyoming, which means about 15 years ago, they'd take a spent nag into the woods between Cody and Yellowstone Park and shoot it. Then they'd stake the dead horse to the ground with ropes, because a big grizzly will bury his kill, and they'd create a cul de sac of dead fall and timber, so the bear could only go out the way he came in. Then they might sit down with a few bottles of Great Falls Select, which used to be a Montana beer, and wait.

Such a trap was called a bear-bait.

Last October, veteran woodsmen Terry Poulsen and Jim Baker took a six-point elk in a little bear-bait clearing north of Sunlight Basin, near Blacktail Creek. Before the two had dressed out the elk, it became dark, and they had not brought a flashlight. Poulsen stooped to light a fire with a match and toilet paper. Baker was sitting on the elk, carving shoulder meat. The rest of the carcass was cut and rolled and ready to pack out. They heard a thump. Baker swiveled to see a grizzly charging full bore down the slope.

101

"He did four jumps, with his fur rolling with each jump, and he covered 20 yards in about 3 seconds. I said, 'Oh, shit.'"

Baker screamed, "Get out of here you son of a bitch!" and this stopped the bear. "He probably hadn't smelled a human amongst all the blood. There was blood all over us."

Baker jumped over the elk but landed in the gut pile of congealed blood, and his feet went out from under him. The bear seemed confused by all the hysteria. The horses, tied tight and high, were going nuts, pounding a hole in the dirt with their hooves, squealing and trying to get away.

"I probably got stepped on two or three times, but I didn't feel it," Baker remembers. "The adrenalin was pumping."

He grabbed his rifle off the horse, reloaded and fired one-handed, pistol-style, into the trees where the bear had last been. The shot lit up the pocket of timber like a flare. It was a night without moon or stars, pitch black. There was the bear, a big one, 4½ to 5 feet at the shoulder, perhaps 500 pounds, the hunters estimated. The grizzly was not intimidated. But he ambled up the slope a few yards. Then he turned.

Poulsen and Baker jumped on the horses. "Grab the antlers, Terry!" Poulsen slid off, but the panicked horse would not let him back on. Baker grabbed the antlers and held Poulsen's horse by the reins. Poulsen swung back up and took the antlers. It was 1000 feet up and a half mile out of the trap. The horses didn't blow till the top. The hunters didn't stop for another hour and a half.

"God, I love life!" shouted Jim Poulsen when they broke out of the timber.

But their dressed elk was now somebody else's hors d'oeuvres. The tables had been turned, at the bottom of the old bear-bait, with Brer Grizzly setting the cloth this time around, a sign, some say, for the '90s. Since Lewis and Clark's day, the grizzly has been hunted and baited. Now the law is to protect the bear as an officially endangered species. Yet grizzlies are not exactly spotted owls.

Last fall, the Wyoming Game and Fish Department confirmed seven reports of grizzlies separating hunters from their elk kills, an unprecedented number, along with many more human–bear encounters, including one where a music teacher felled a 450-pound charging female with one lucky shot through the spine from a closing distance of 7 feet, Meriwether Lewis style. Around Cody, Terry Poulsen and Jim Baker are known as "The Griz Buddies," and elk-snatching bears are being called "Dinner Bell Grizzlies."

Are grizzlies really coming to the sound of gunshots like dogs responding to the supper chime? "A 30.06 can be a poor learning experience, when it's aimed at them," says Doug Peacock, author of *Grizzly Years*, "or a signal for a reward, if it's aimed at something else, like an elk. They can learn the difference quickly."

"We don't like to excite the public unnecessarily," cautions Craig Fax of Wyoming Game and Fish. "It may just be that there's a bear in the immediate area. It responds to the disturbance. Might be the horses, the commotion, not necessarily the shots."

This is cutting a fine line, as to reward signal. Others are skeptical about the whole business. "Dinner bell grizzlies is stretching it a bit, though recent studies show these bears are as smart as chimpanzees," says Lewis Robinson III, the impresario who recently opened the Grizzly Discovery Center in West Yellowstone.

Bears have always keyed in on gut piles, of course. Why so many encounters now? After all, the 100,000 buffalo-chomping kings of the prairie that Lewis and Clark grew to respect have been reduced in Greater Yellowstone to about 230 to 450 (still not so shy) mountain dwellers.

Those who say that the grizzly habitat is constantly being chipped away by industrial tourism and ranchette development on the edges of Yellowstone argue, strongly, that the rash of sightings has been caused by a poor food year at the higher elevations. Wet conditions hurt the huckleberry and chokecherry crops. There were no white pine nuts, and the balls of high-protein cutworm moth larvae, which grizzlies hit like canapes at a film festival, did not materialize.

"As many as 50 grizzlies in different locations feed on these huge caches of cutworms," explains Dave Moody, Large Predator Coordinator for Game and Fish.

As a result, what grizzlies there are moved down to human level. However, a minority view holds that the grizzly population is rising. (The total number in North America, including Alaska, is about 800.) "Nobody would say there are less than ten years ago," Fax believes. "Protection has had something to do with that."

If the numbers are indeed up, these folks argue it may be time to start thinking about delisting *Ursus horribilis* as an endangered species.

"It's time to start shooting grizzlies again," say Poulsen and Baker. "We need to put the fright back in them. These bears are not pussycats."

Peacock, who became legendary for living among grizzlies while he put his head back together after two tours in Vietnam as a Green Beret medic, believes the solution is to designate wildlife corridors so that the bears can move in and out of Yellowstone, Glacier, and other habitat "islands."

"We're getting ready to take dams off some of our rivers. Why not re-create wilderness for the grizzlies? It's time to take a shot at people living with them."

Unlike many environmentalists, Peacock does not oppose bear hunts. "I just believe in giving them a sporting chance," he says. "The hunting weapons of the twentieth century are so powerful they can bring down a B-52. I advocate hunting with javelins—that's the right direction, swords, perhaps. The last time I was in polar bear country, I took a spear. That's real sporting."

An early season spear hunt in Wyoming would probably be a good thing. Serious hunters should support it. I'm sure the grizzlies would.

But between allowing grizzlies to have all the berries they can get their claws on in an expanded system of wildlife corridors and humbling them with 180-grain elk load lies a third solution, the most controversial of all. This is to incarcerate the problem grizzlies in "habitats" (don't say "zoos") such as Lewis Robinson's $50-million Grizzly Discovery Center. A problem grizzly may best be defined as one who has a tendency to dine upon menstruating backpackers in place of, or in addition to, cutworm moths.

The center is a manicured 87-acre affair sited only 100 yards from the west entrance to Yellowstone. The grizzlies are kept in 1-acre pens that resemble vest pocket parks in Switzerland, with treats of peanut butter and blueberries hidden here and there so that tourists on the other side of a moat can watch the bears forage. At dinner time, yes, a bell is rung. I have visited, and although I am no bear psychologist and have never encountered a grizzly on or about my own 20 acres in the Beartooths north of Sunlight Basin (my dry cleaner would know if I had), I guessed the bears looked happy enough, though maybe bored. Their claws have been taken out.

"The place is a monument to the tame and domestic," fumes Peacock. "If it was somewhere else it might be OK, but Yellowstone Park is the closest thing we've got to the true wild. One of the reasons grizzlies have value is that they are free. It's enough to know they are there. Boatloads of Japanese tourists don't need to see them."

If Peacock represents the "Free Willy" point of view, others, neighbors in West Yellowstone, cite *Jurassic Park*. To all, the cheerful Robinson counters, in effect, "Better Fed than Dead." His first stellar exhibit, a bear named Fred (after Fred Smith, who runs Federal Express), was overnighted from the Denali region of Alaska after he drew a death sentence for menacing one too many mining camps.

However, points out Moody, the biologist, "You might as well kill the captive bears. They have been neutered and will never again contribute to the gene pool."

This may be what rankles Peacock the most, too. Remove the "predatory, dominant animals, bears who for some reason have less fear of man"—in other words, the dinner bell grizzlies—and with time, at least in Peacock's opinion, "the genetic composition of the population will shift and we will be left with an animal who looks like a grizzly, albeit a small one, but whose behavior will more closely resemble that of the meeker black bear."

No one knows whether in the coming fall dinner bell grizzlies will return to human level or stay in the high country to chew their beloved cutworms. Recovering all grizzlies, as a species, in order to hunt them or just to know they are there, wild and wily, will take generations. Creating corridors and living with the largest predator in America is not a quick-fix procedure, like banning DDT in order to bring back eagles. On the other hand, if we decide to say the hell with it and head the other way, perhaps delisting is a form of ecocide best accomplished slowly—with a spear.

Tarpon Jihad

Hundred-twenty-pound tarpon jumps into the boat. Thrashes about. Breaks the client's leg. Jumps back into Florida Bay wearing a deck chair for a necktie. Evidently, these fellows are not brook trout.

As we pole, *sotto voce*, into position, Sid Bryant, the guide, explains the eccentricities of our prey. Gills rattle like tin cans. Tarpon get to flying horizontal. Tail-walking is only the first book of the Bible. In actual point of fact, certain tarpon have been noted 6 feet above the Gulf Stream talking to Los Angeles on the cellular, says Mr. Bryant, and I believe him. When the shrimp move through the Keys on a warm night in June, the sound of these scaly dogs busting the surface is like God dropping bowling balls on the ocean from heaven. It's violent, it's visual. Tarpon are lions. Sid whispers: "The only thing missing is *roar.*"

But I don't have to be convinced. I am seriously juiced. This is like the time in the Holiday Inn in Billings when I was 17 and so was she, and she started to peel back the creased white hotel sheet with such a deliberate display of slow insouciance that I knew, standing there, that the experience was going to be far better than even I could imagine it.

First time out.

What I am trying to say is 10 tarpon are already circling the boat. Bryant, originally from Georgia, is not just whistling Dixie here. We're the center of the clock, and they're the ticking, reptilian fish cutting the smooth stone surface all around us, rolling across the flats, inexorably closer. Makes me sweat, and that's on top of the weather, which is beyond balmy for a Montana boy who was skating the ice of the frozen creek behind the house a couple days back. This morning, Hurricane Edouard lies across our noses like some troublesome French tickler, 235 miles south-by-southeast, or so sayeth the Weather Channel.

Problem is, the tarpon are not biting. They're smiling. That girl back at the Holiday Inn (now a mother of three, and for all I know, probably the holder of several Internet access patents), she was smiling, too. But tarpon, I don't know if that strange side-swipe gash of a bucket-mouth they were born with can ever be said to portray true mirth. The girl in the Holiday Inn was sincere. It is possible these tarpon may not be.

At this point, I am not sure if I care to ascribe intelligence to what is in all actuality no more than a giant sardine, largest member of the herring family.

Softly, like the jingle of a reindeer's harness, the little live pilcher at the end of my line turns twitchety.

"Don't do a thing!" Sid shouts, whispers, and commands at the same time. "Let 'er come tight."

I don't and it does.

"Wait'll he turns, then strike him good; tarpon has a jaw like a brick, don't forget now to bow to the King!"

 The guides call the west side of the Florida Keys, fronting the Ever-glades off Isla Morada, The Backyard. Minus many tall mountains, it reminds me of my own backyard, only underwater, an endless flooded pasture of waving aquarium grass with all manner of barnyard creatures crawling about in plain view: rays, sharks, bones, herds of baitfish, tarpon. You want to take the net and just jump out of the boat and fork 'em. Yet—this would be wrong.

I say this with some bitterness because the hook has just pulled free. I reel in. Sid examines one dead pilcher, my former bait. Probably died of fright.

"Dang, look at the teeth marks. It was a shark. Those guys are Gumby."

Meanwhile, the tarpon have passed us by. Their tails wave back at us like Esther Williams, while three nurse sharks seem to have taken a liking to our boat.

Shark-infested waters. Little guys, 3 feet or so, but I wouldn't want them gumming my ankles.

Sid says, no longer quite whispering, "I've been in the midst of hundreds of rolling tarpon, tried every bait known to man, and nothing works. Are they feeding on something else? No, they're just done feeding."

It's a bad sign when the guide starts asking questions of the wind during a calm, and worse when he begins to soliloquize.

"It's awful tough to start up that boat," continues Sid, "move to another spot, when you see tarpon rollin' all around you like here, 'cause you might not see another fish, next four spots you stop. But 89° is hot enough to boil lobsters."

Sid's ahead of me on this tarpon thing. He's leaning over, studying the water thermometer. Edouard, that sucky little Gallic blow, is beating us to the boards. Tarpon won't bite if the water's too hot.

So we rocket out to a place called Barne's Key, which looks, as we approach, like a silk pillow floating on a jade sea so limpid it could be the fluid in your lover's eye. I really don't care if the water's too hot for fishing, not now (though I hate to be beaten by a sardine). Instantly, this place reminds me of the Holiday Inn.

We cast about.

"There's some bones," says Sid, as a platoon of translucent suckers comes marching fashionably toward us.

I suppose there are those among us who would switch to bonefishing, about now.

"The assignment's for tarpon," I say.

"Well," says Sid, "if we don't see tarpon right about now, right here, then we're kidding ourselves."

Ten AM and it's over. Sun's burning us up. Moon offers scant shade.

PREDATOR ALLEY

Next morning, dawn, as usual.

We scoot through Channel 2 to Indian Key, then do Channel 5, which takes us off Long Key, searching for tails.

We anchor, and the talk is good.

"This place is notorious for sharks and 'cudas hitting the prey," whispers Sid, and I admit, looking over the neck of pass current, and also down at the great grey brow of Edouard looming up on us to the south, that I wouldn't want to fall out of the boat just now. But the tarpon seem to have gone north, probably sipping blue margaritas in some pastel bistro in South Beach, Miami, muscling their way to the bar, with their big goggle eyes and that conspicuous lack of shoulders. Tarpon take a 42 long. Very long.

The waters off Long Key are beginning to remind me of the Great Salt Lake. Nothing can live here. Sometimes, fishing, you get a feel for a hole. Either it's going to be outrageous, or it's going to be pitiful.

So far, I've learned everything about tarpon but how to release them.

THE CLUB MED OF TARPON

In fishing as in life, it is often best to admit defeat and move as quickly as possible, by cover of night if need be, to happier hunting grounds. My mother lives a couple hours drive north of Isla Morada and a jog around Miami, at the WinDixie epicenter of a town called Stuart. Stuart happens to be the official self-proclaimed "Sailfish Capital of the World." During the last Prohibition, it was also home to William "Bill" "The Real" McCoy, who smuggled the best scotch then available. Stuart holds the world record for sea trout, for snook, and for African pompano, too. There's a marina I like to frequent, Pirate's Cove Resort, which is built of such staunch stucco and cement that I believe it might withstand even a French hurricane.

Though my mother's condominium lies only 5 minutes away, I am reluctant to go fishing with her, since, at 93, her best tarpon days may be behind her. However, since tarpon-fishing is best at dawn, and my mother is probably best at lunch, I think I can get the business done before noon, after which the sharper colors, in life as in Florida, begin to spoil, anyway. From Pirate's Cove, the tarpon grounds are easily accessible. You roll out of bed and take the elevator down to the dock.

"Where we going first?" I ask Capt. Warren Gorall.

"The Club Med."

Capt. Gorall, an older gentleman, scares me in his brevity. But he gets the job done. Thing I like about a good guide, *Capitão* Gorall or Sid Bryant, is they don't jet-boat you around the tulies. They know where the fish are. If they're there, they tell you how to whack 'em. If they're not, you're back at the dock by breakfast, crying in your curried eggs.

We boat out to the Club Med, an upscale compound just as you may envision it, minus topless Parisians, since this is Florida. The estuary narrows here. Palms rise above the mangroves. Australian pines are scattered between capacious houses with capacious bug screens surrounding capacious swimming pools. The water is brown but translucent, lusciously so, to my way of thinking, since half a dozen tarpon are scooching about, sucking up invertebrates.

Captain Gorall suggests that my son Cody, 7 years old and along for the ride, cast his bobber and shrimp just about anywhere.

"Bounce it off the bottom; don't worry about hanging up."

Then Gorall gets serious with the paying charter. Hooks me up with a 9-weight fly rod, balanced with a 9-weight line, at which point the 7-year-old announces, "My bobber's gone."

We investigate. I hate tarpon. Cicadas blast away in the Australian pines. There exists no longer a shrimp at the end of the kid's line.

The tarpons tail closer to the Med, spurning our advances like girl dolphins in a cross-species Brazilian movie.

Capt. Gorall takes my rod and cranks it bitterly. "Forget it. They're down. That was history."

 On the way out to the narrow jetty where the Atlantic meets the Saint Lucie Inlet, Gorall explains about double-hauling, how to pull back the heavy line

with your left hand while you move the rod forward to 10 o'clock with your right, and about how it's slow and jerky for tarpon and fast for barracuda, when Cody shouts: "Dolphins!" and we pause in deep water off a drawbridge as seven or eight bottlenoses cruise us, and I know we are having fun yet, though fishless. Already the trooper, Gorall says, "See those tarpon? Cast to midnight."

Seems like these tarpon guys can't get enough of us. I mean, we're at 60 fathoms, the dolphins are still smiling, and over by midnight is a new pod of silver pigs, tailing. I cast, with a studied clumsiness. They dive.

"Yes," says Captain Gorall. What he means to say is, "Fuggit!"

At the rock jetty entrance to the Atlantic, we fish the last of the incoming tide, hence the captain's urgency.

I cast something called a Terror-Eyez, in a root beer color, manufactured by a local company called D.O.A.

Later, Gorall will explain: "You see the tarpon coming toward you, you cast 5, 6 feet in front, start to strip back from him, since nothing littler than him ever goes anywhere else but away, and he speeds up, and buckets da bait!"

I remember that night at the Holiday Inn. She didn't exactly tail-walk, though. That was love. This is obsession. The tarpon grabs the plastic and jumps clean out of the water. My firstborn son is goggle-eyed and I'm cranking. Four-foot sardine tail-walks right at us, and this was a short cast, 10 yards.

I should explain to you that the tarpon fell on my line and broke it. Gorall sighs.

"Like I said, next time, bow to the king."

How to do it addendum: The tarpon walks across the water upon her tail, you best bow the rod to the salt, give her the slack, or your leader is Gumby.

Bow to the king, or chew fried eggs.

Snowboarding
Waikiki

This is one of those stories that start out to be one thing and end up something else. Two years ago I was doing a magazine piece about the hard-on surf culture of Hawaii's North Shore. A model named Cindy Crawford had already had her pictures taken with the local boys in a Woody van, and somebody had to explain to New York what a wave was. The last surfer I talked with was the most famous of them all, and by far the oldest, George Downing. Downing, then 60, had won every major surf contest. He had been world champion three times. In fact, it was a 1955 newspaper photograph of Downing (with Buzzy Trent and Woody Brown) cascading down a 20-foot steamroller in his—insane! controlled! casual!—style that had first brought California surfers, agog, to the islands, long before there ever were surf contests. And Downing's roots went back much further. He was a fourth generation white Hawaiian who had been tutored by the legendary beach boys, Steamboat Mokuahi, Brownie Barnes, and Duke Kahanamoku himself, Olympic star of wave and screen, the man who introduced surfing to California and Australia in the 1920s.

Standing in Downing's custom surfboard shop and Get Wet! fashion factory in downtown Honolulu, I expected him to be one macho waterman. For days, Pt. Break kids young enough to be Downing's grandchildren had been waxing my ears with stories of the ultimate wipe-out, their idea of a near-death experience beneath mountains of foam. I asked Downing, who looks more like an anthropology professor than a surf legend, if he had ever come close to drowning himself.

121

"Oh," said Downing, rolling his hands, "I know what I can't do, and I don't do it."

That put everybody else into perspective.

"Surfing's simple," he said. "It's a matter of balance."

I wanted to ask him if he was kidding, but he stared me down with his smile.

"Come back to Honolulu sometime," he added. "I'll teach you how to surf."

 Waikiki, March 24, 199–, high noon. It is hot. Japanese girls in bikinis flounce into outriggers. There are 10,000 people within a few strokes of a sea kayak. Behind us is the 10-foot municipal statue of Duke Kahanamoku, the patron saint of Waikiki. Downing's buddies, the last surviving beachboys of Honolulu, look me over. They have names like Captain Bob and J. R. They have potbellies below their still considerable muscles and black-out glasses above. They are cordial and menacing at the same time. They grant me respect, because I am with George.

But George, since I saw him last, has become the reluctant professor.

"I don't want to be on the cover of some magazine. My life is not important. I will talk to you in the context of saving Waikiki. Then maybe we can surf some."

I want to arrange a simple afternoon of narcissism. George wants to save the oceans. I've never been on a surfboard in my life, and learning to surf with Downing promises to be like taking a screen test with Jack Nicholson as acting coach.

What George is worried about—outraged by,

would be a better way of putting it—are the artificial reefs that have been installed in Mamala Bay, in front of Waikiki about a mile offshore, by Atlantis Submarines. The reefs are composed of an abandoned Navy ship, several airplanes, and a steel structure of staggered pedestals. This engaging flotsam serves to attract colorful reef fish, which can be viewed by tourists through submarine portholes 100 feet down. Atlantis divers had been feeding the little fish dried dog food to induce them to populate the new reefs. Though Waikiki enjoys several dozen high-rise hotels ("concrete trees," Downing calls them) and millions of tourists, its waters are not so good at producing coral, and coral is necessary to attract reef fish.

The problem, as Downing sees it, is that little reef fish attract larger open-water fish, and these fish may lure sharks, some small, such as black-tips, and others not so small, such as tiger sharks. Last year a tiger shark had bled one surfer to death off the North Shore, on the far side of the island, and created a practical concern among the powers that be in Honolulu, who then organized a Shark Task Force to hunt tigers. Nobody had yet seen a tiger off Waikiki, and no bathers or surfers had been bitten, but much of Oahu was nervous, especially George and the members of the powerful environmental organization he is a leader of, Save Our Surf.

"Waikiki is justly famous as the most peaceful ocean setting on earth. What if some Japanese tourist were to be attacked by a shark?" asks George. "A little $50 million a year business like Atlantis Submarines could bring about the downfall of a 5 billion business, the hotel and tourist industry of Honolulu. You can't sail away a hotel like a submarine!"

J. R. brings over the board I will be using, which is a knockoff of one Downing designed 30 years before. This classic axe is long and thick enough to float an elephant in a riptide.

"J. R., I think Steve is going to be a friend of ours," says George. "If not, well, he won't show his face on this beach again. Remember what happened to Captain Cook."

"George," I have to laugh, "You know I went out on the submarine ride this morning to see if there were any sharks. I've got to be fair."

"Fuck being fair!" Downing shouts, then smiles. "In life there is no purgatory. There is heaven and there is hell. Nothing in between! You be fair in whatever you write, but you lean a little bit, you know, to our side. Remember Captain Cook."

J. R. smiles.

"Look at that creature," says George, distracted. "Yoi, yoi!"

The creature is a wide-bodied Japanese tourist about 19 years old with a bottom a sumo wrestler could love.

"Surfing!" says George, snapping back. "Catching a wave is like—. Anybody can do it. But riding a wave, that's like making love. You caress the wave. Take its pulse. Learn its personality."

I guess that the lesson has begun. But, no, George leans against the big upright board.

"There was this girl in the old days—she was beautiful—and she would tattoo your name on the inside of her thigh if she enjoyed making love to you, like, 'GEORGE WAS HERE.' Her thighs had all these stenciled notes!" He laughs. "And she would shout out of the window of the bus as she passed down Kalakaua Avenue, 'George, you're the best! He's the best! Everybody! It's George!' And I'd be so embarrassed, I was just a kid. She wasn't no whore, she was just cool."

Downing smiles me down again.

"These artificial reefs are a direct threat to my way of life, you understand. I don't take kindly to that. I'm a metaphor."

The man is calling himself a metaphor, and we haven't gotten wet yet.

"OK," says George. "Surfing. Surfing's simple."

George sets the big board down on the sand, lies across it, tells me to scoot up 6 inches from the end, tells me that when I stand up my hands shouldn't be placed too far in front of my shoulders or too far behind, demonstrates, stands up as a small crowd recognizes him. Myself, I feel a little out of place. I feel like a pasty *haoli*, or foreigner. I get the feeling George never feels out of place. Of course, Waikiki is his living room.

"Keep it simple," says George. "That's the point."

"Casual."

"Casual," says George, who is the King of Casual.

Terry O'Halloran, general manager of Atlantis Divers and representative of Atlantis Submarines, does not view Downing casually.

"What do you think of George Downing's opposition to your artificial reefs?" I ask him.

"George is one of the grand masters of surfing in Hawaii and deserves a lot of credit for that—"

"But what do you think of him?"

"I just told you."

O'Halloran sighs, and I feel sorry for him. Downing is to Hawaii what Pele is to Brazil or Nicholson is to Hollywood. How do you fight a folk legend? The last time Downing testified to the state legislature against underwater fish-feeding, he read a poem he had composed the night before, in English and Hawaiian. Television stations covered his testimony.

"Obviously, we have a different opinion from Downing," says O'Halloran. "We term artificial reefs *reef enhancement*. In the past, pesticides and other pollutants were allowed to essentially kill the environment off Waikiki. Our reefs bring back marine life. Already coral 5 to 6 inches high is growing on our sunken ship. The ocean is now claiming these structures. We feel that is not bad, but desirable.

"We are an example of eco-tourism. Our submarines are electric and nonpolluting. You can't throw trash out the portholes. We educate our passengers that this is a special marine environment that needs a lot of protection."

Atlantis has 200 employees and carries 225,000 passengers a year. Aquatic tourism, as it is called, is growing at a time when Oahu's hotel occupancy is falling. The Save Our Surf organization would like the reefs to be moved far from Waikiki, but their location so close to the hotels is what makes the Atlantis operation so easily profitable.

O'Halloran believes there is "an atmosphere of fear" based on the recent tiger shark attacks off the North Shore and off Maui. "This is a long way from us. The Shark Task Force has caught some 29 tigers off the North Shore, but none near our reefs. The task force nets off Waikiki give no evidence there are tigers here, which is not to say we don't have sharks in these waters. But it is not as if the reefs attracted them."

O'Halloran says the company has voluntarily stopped fish-feeding of dog food, after being asked to by the Hawaiian Department of Natural Resources. He stresses, "From January to now May, we've seen sharks only 25% of the time. The most common type is a white- or black-tipped reef shark. We've never seen a tiger shark out there."

On the short catamaran cruise from the dock in front of the Hilton to the meet with the white Atlantis submarine over the artificial reefs, I read a company brochure: "Climb aboard and you're set for a once-in-a-lifetime journey through Hawaii's natural undersea world. Come face to face with 'puhi,' Hawaii's feared moray eels. See why the 'humuhu-munukunukuapua'a' is nicknamed the 'Picasso fish.' Witness the docile behavior of manta rays and the circling nature of the awesome shark!"

All 60 or so passengers are Japanese, except for me. We are guided to our seats in front of the portholes by cleanly smiling guides in white uniforms. The slow descent is strangely thrilling. The air is pressurized, there are no bumps or ahh-oog-ahs! and then we are smoothing along the sandy bottom.

I don't know if I'm just lucky, but a black-tipped reef shark soon fins over to the porthole. His name, says the guide, is "Nigel." Nigel is about 5 feet long, not the sort of guest you would invite over for crab cocktails, but a critter I had swum within yards of many times while scuba diving off neighboring islands.

Downing cites evidence that black-tips are responsible for many shark bites off Florida, while the Atlantis guide assures me Nigel and his fellows are harmless. At a Shark Task Force meeting last year, Jean-Michel Cousteau stated that creating a situation which attracted large numbers of fish and their predators close to shore was "a disaster waiting to happen."

No awesome sharks beneath our surfboards at the moment. Finally, we're off the beach and on the waves, Downing and I, conducting a sort of mid-ocean interview. These waves are about 6 feet, measured seaside. Everybody seems to be waiting for something bigger. This piece of ocean, called Queens Break, a quarter mile off the center of Waikiki, is like an exclusive blue country club. There aren't many surfers here, and a few even seem recognizable from ABC's Wide World of Sports. All look highly competent, with one exception.

People wave to George from their boards. Young guys signal with a bit of embarrassment. A Hawaiian woman in her early 30s paddles close. She is the only woman out. "What is this, George? Legends day at Queens?"

George nods, but quickly commands: "Turn around. Don't try to stand up. I'll push you. Go."

There is no time to be afraid. I'm rocketing along like a freight train that's jumped the tracks. Speed creates its own stability. From the corner of my eye, I can see the woman. She is carving the face of the wave with her much smaller modern board, climbing the foam, pirouetting, whapping the nose first right than left. She drives right over to me, and over the roar of the curl she says: "Good." Then she disappears like a dolphin.

It takes me minutes to paddle back out to George.

"What did you do wrong?" asks George.

"I got scared?"

"No. You did great. But what don't you do on the freeway?"

I'm thinking.

"You don't drive the wrong way."

"On the freeway?"

"Paddling back, you went through the surf line, the other surfers who are waiting for their waves. That's not good. That makes some people mad."

In other words, if I wasn't with George and I did what I just did at Queens Break, definitely a locals-only kind of place, I might be pummeled to mango meat like Keanu Reeves when he met the surf bikers in *Point Break.*

"What a day!" says George, to take the edge off. "I learned everything I know here. I owe everything to this beach."

When he was 8, George used to sleep under the palms in front of the Duke statue, after his family broke up. He was a street kid on the most beautiful street in the world, Waikiki.

Of course, he says, he was a good kid, polite to everybody, beachcombers, whores, and millionaires. A famous waterman—which in old Honolulu meant a beach boy who could paddle, surf, fish, play the ukelele, and romance the tourists with equal *casual*—took George under his wing. This was Steamboat Mokuahi. Steamboat had a friendly fishing rivalry going with Judge Steiner. Judge Steiner owned three mansions where the 45-story Hyatt Waikiki now stands, cutting off our view of the soaring razor mountains behind. But Judge Steiner was not as accomplished an angler as Steamboat Mokuahi. He couldn't cast his line as far. One day, the Judge took George aside and said, "George, maybe you could figure out a way to get my line out farther than Steamboat's."

So, every day about sunset, when Steiner and Steamboat would be fishing, George would happen to take out his board. When he walked by the Judge, he would pick up the hook between his toes, and tow the line out as he paddled to Queens. The Judge suddenly started to catch more bonefish than Steamboat.

One day Uncle Benny, who was the cabbie that

ran all the professional girls on this part of the beach, took George aside.

"You know, for some reason, Judge Steiner likes you."

"He does?"

"Yeah, he does. You should ask him to let you sleep in one of his houses."

"What do you mean?"

"Well, George, every night you sleepin' on the beach. Across the street, the Judge owns three houses. Ask him."

George did, and the Judge said, "Sure, George. But you keep my lawns in good order."

So now George is sleeping in the basement of a mansion on Waikiki. He has to keep his buddies off the lawn, but no coconuts are falling on his head, and Judge Steiner is a good man to know, for a street kid in Honolulu, in the old days.

George is learning. Everything. With surfing in first place. One night he shows up late for his ukelele lesson with Brownie Barnes and the beachboys. George was surfing at night, something the guys sometimes did naked to freak the tourists dressing for dinner in the rooms of the old Royal Hawaiian Hotel. Barnes takes him aside, and George thinks he's in for it. But Brownie says, "George, the boys and I have decided that you will be our world champion."

George is speechless.

"Come here," says Brownie. Brownie takes him to his beach locker, where rows of humongous classic surfboards still stand in Honolulu's municipal surf rack, and hands George his own competition redwood board. George has never owned a board worth more than $5, and it took him weeks to pay for that one. Brownie's board is worth hundreds, in pre-World War II dollars.

George is close to tears now. But he does, eventually, become the world's champion.

"These people, the artificial reef people," says George, sitting cross-legged on his board as the waves rumble under us, "they do what they do for money, not for the ocean, not for the people. They have no *aloha!*"

In George Downing's mouth, *aloha* is not just the name of an airline. *Aloha*, to him, is the kindness of strangers who helped out a homeless street kid long ago. *Aloha* is what Honolulu is or was or should be all about. *Aloha* is love, and if you don't get that, get off the beach.

"It's like this," says George, all the while cocking an eye for the next good wave, "the people who work in these hotels"—he sweeps a hand across the skyscraper run of Waikiki, between Diamond Head and the airport—"they don't make much money. They used to live on the beach. Now they live in housing projects an hour's drive from town, in traffic. And you want to take away their ocean?" George's face turns dark. "The old people who grew up here will be sad. The young people will see them grieving. They will become bitter, and this is not a good situation."

George shrugs.

"You know," he says, "when a wave hits the shore, it doesn't stop. The energy of that wave keeps going, all the way through the island, through the ocean on the other side, around the world until a new wave is formed from the old. Don't mess—" he grabs the nose of my board, and turns it around, interrupting himself, "Take this wave, it's a good one, stand up, remember what I told you, don't think!" I paddle like a madman, and George shouts after me, "Don't mess with the *aloha!*"

I do stand up. It's like riding a washing machine with the door open, but soon I notice Captain Bob is riding alongside, holding a camera in one hand and, for occasional balance, poking a broken canoe paddle into the crest with the other. While I wobble for dear life, Captain Bob snaps clear picture after clear picture.

So I got to be a wave rider, when all I wanted to do was to learn to surf. I don't know if George set up the luminaries on the waves at Queens, asked them to show up that afternoon and become reinforcement for the story. I wonder about it.

After our last wave, we walked down Waikiki to the New Otami Hotel, where the locals hang out, since it has the best sunset. And there we just happened to run into Rick Bernstein, the 6′ 3″ swimmer who started the whole concern about the new reefs. Bernstein is a Hatha yoga teacher who swims 5 miles along Waikiki every day. One sunset he got to thinking about a mile off shore, where the water is very deep and very blue, that he didn't like worrying while he swam that a shark might get him, a shark attracted to Waikiki by fish-feeding for the tourists. Back on shore, he called up George: "George, we got a problem with Waikiki." George said, "I'll be right over."

And over drinks at the Otami bar, we just happened to run into Whitney Anderson, who helped to carry George's anti-fish-feeding bill in the legislature. The Hawaiian legislature decided to recommend an end to fish-feeding off Waikiki and to begin a study that would determine whether artificial reefs posed a threat to surfers and bathers.

Old beach boys like George leave nothing up to chance because they believe so strongly in coincidence. Coincidence has taken them off the beach, made them rich, made them famous. The wave hits the shore, travels around the world, and becomes the wave again.

"I hate competition," says George when he drops me off at the airport. "I hate to see anyone lose, in love, in business, in sport." Long pause. Stare. "On the other hand, I know how to win."

Last Fish

I knew it was a slow day on the Yellowstone because we had been casting and changing flies for almost an hour and my father had not hooked a thing.

I hadn't caught any trout either, but I had lower expectations. I was 14, and I was a bait and lures fisherman. It was cold that day along the river inside the Park. Patches of dirty snow still rested against the shady sides of the pines and in the cups of the white granite rocks. The river was high and wide and green-brown. I wanted to rig up the little three-hook worm contraptions we had used to knock the rainbows dead the weekend before up on Checkerboard Creek, where the roaring June stream chunked away the bank and the worms too as the water ripped through the level fields.

That was meat fishing. Now we were only a few miles below Yellowstone Lake, and, as the metal signs clearly read, this was strictly a "Catch-and-Release," "Fly-Fishing Only" area. My father was zinging little size 18 snowflies into the ripples and trying home-tied nymphs, but my snowflies seemed to sink and my nymphs quickly snagged bottom. I was considering edging downstream and slipping a good redworm over my snowfly. The bait was in a sawed-off milk carton behind the cooler in the back seat.

I turned upstream to see how far my father was standing from our new Chevrolet when I noticed a car pulling alongside. It was a Chevy too but a lot older, the hump-backed 1954 model. This brown car sniffed alongside ours like a grizzly bear and then

Author's Note: That's the way it was in 1959.

bumped gently across the dirt ridge separating the parking area from the sloping bank. The car loped right on down. The muddy wheels rose and dipped in the recently thawed ground until the car came to rest beside my father, not 2 feet away from the river.

I ran over. Grown men didn't drive their cars to the edge of the Yellowstone, even in Wyoming.

"Got any worms?" asked the driver cool enough.

The man looked normal, if tired. He was a brown-leather cowboy in his late 50s, perhaps early 60s: frayed but clean snap-button shirt, blue jeans, scuffed red-brown boots. He rolled down the window in the cold and smiled with yellow plug tobacco teeth. My father looked past him into the back seat. So did I.

There, hunkered down and as grizzled as a poor man's version of the terminal Howard Hughes, was a razor-faced man about the same age as the driver. The man in back was layered in green Army blankets and an old wool great-coat with a fur collar. His gray eyes were so sunken that bones were about all there was to be seen on his face except for a hand-rolled cigarette that was pushed out of the corner of his mouth like a hot thermometer. Beside him on the seat was a beat-up little casting rod, rigged with a couple of split shot and an oversized snelled hook, and next to the pole was a folded wooden wheelchair as ancient and decrepit as the car and its passengers.

"Worms?" said my father. "This run is fly-fishing only, and besides, it's catch-and-release all along here."

The driver put up the window and stepped outside. He did not bother to roll down his plaid shirt. The blankets and closed windows were for his friend.

"It's going to be Ike's last fish," said the cowboy. He tested the stubble on his chin with the palm of his hand. Could have raised sparks on that chin.

"What do you mean?" asked my father.

"He's dead. Ike's dead."

We looked in back.

"He's going to be. Got only a few days to go. I drove down to Thermopolis and busted him out of the VA Hospital. I don't think anybody should die in a hospital, do you?"

The man flipped his hand off his chin and jerked his thumb toward the back seat. The old Chevy was filling with cigarette smoke like a poker parlor on Saturday night. The seat looked to be on fire but through the haze we could see Ike busy rolling another smoke as the butt in his mouth almost burned his lips.

"They didn't let him smoke in the hospital," said the driver.

"What's he dying of?" father asked.

"Lung cancer."

The driver coughed a couple times himself, more from the cold, I figured. He clapped his shoulders and stamped on the wet ground.

"So's you got any worms?"

"Yeah," I said real quick, speaking for the first time. "I got 'em behind the cooler."

My father watched me run over to our car.

"I guess we could loan you a few. Little red worms."

"I don't care if they're ringworms."

I came back with a good handful.

Ike's friend opened the back door and took out the pole. He picked a worm out of my hand and baited up the big hook. He did this in a funny way. He clipped the worm in short segments with his dirty fingernails and slid them over the hook onto the leader. Then he did the same with two more worms, covering the hook and half an inch of leader with solid wriggling worm shank.

"Ike's not going to be good for too many casts, I bet," he said. "We gonna present these Yellowstone trout with a Dagwood sandwich they cannot pass up."

He set the rod across the hood and we set to work getting old Ike out of the car. Ike didn't weigh much more anymore but what he did weigh had to be lifted by us alone.

Father and the driver crossed their arms under Ike, and I rolled out the rickety wheelchair. I set the chair close to the car but my father looked at the straight running water in front of us and said, "Let's carry him around the corner by the pines. That's the good spot. That's the best place."

We got Ike set up in front of the pool like a king on his throne. The driver stuck the glass pole in Ike's hand, and Ike pulled the cigarette out of his mouth to survey the water professionally.

I didn't know if he was strong enough to cast.

"You want me to toss it out for you, Sir?" I asked.

He looked at me vacant and cold. Then a slow-starting smile began to wash across his face like a paintbrush sweeping the bottom of a duck decoy until he was as close to laughing as he was ever going to come again.

"Whatsa matter, boy? You think I'm sick or something?"

Ike had a sense of humor, but the humor was too much for him. He pulled in the cigarette and crossed the rod over the arms of the chair and started to cough and cough and rack his throat out horribly. None of us reached out to help him. He didn't drop the pole—or the cigarette, either.

"Want me to roll you a smoke?" Ike asked my dad, almost smiling again.

"That's OK," said my father.

Ike cocked the pole over his right shoulder with both hands.

It looked to me that if he shot his line way out in the center he would surely fall out of the chair.

This must have occurred to Ike, too.

"I reckon," he wheezed, "there's always more fish close to the bank than there ever is out in the middle. Everybody's always trying to fish the far bank, if you know what I mean. I reckon there's more fish close to home than anywhere else."

Nobody said anything to that, so Ike sort of flipped the rod to the right and the worm and sinker plopped down perfectly, about 10 feet upstream, just 2 or 3 feet from the deep bank right about where my father would have thrown his first cast.

The line drifted and nothing happened.

"I wouldn't worry," said Ike to me. "I don't have much time so I know the trout are going to oblige me."

The line drifted level to the rod tip, and Ike took up the slack. He was in perfect position for a strike, and that's just when the fish hit!

The cigarette bobbed in Ike's mouth and he tried the third smile of the cold day.

"Don't keep a dead man waiting, fish," Ike said calmly, setting the hook.

This kind of action beat snowflies and nymphs in my book.

Ike mostly horsed the fish in, but he let it play and jump once too. The smile stayed on his face as the fish leaped all the way out of the water. Color came to Ike's face, and for a few seconds he lost himself in the fishing and strength and health seemed to return to him, but when the fish went under again I could see that Ike did not have muscle left to play him properly. Ike took the chance and quick-reeled his fish toward the bank.

I knew he couldn't reach down himself so I stepped into the icy water to corner the rainbow. It was a pretty good trout too, about 17 inches, but they ran big in this section.

"Hey, kid," said Ike. He took a quick breath with every few words. "I got him. He's my fish. Don't worry. You'll catch cold. Look out. This baby's coming aboard."

And he swung the fish as far up the bank as he could.

That was it for Ike. The rod dropped out of his hands and he fell across the arm of the wheelchair. My dad and Ike's buddy reached down to prop him up. He was all right though. Just exhausted. The lick of a smile lay across the side of his mouth. The cigarette had fallen into the water.

But the rainbow was still going strong. He flipped off the slack line and flopped for the river.

This is where you need a kid at streamside. I charged out of the river and fell across the fish. Didn't get him the first try. The trout squeezed between my arms and I had to bat it up the bank with a slap of my hand and fall across him a second time.

I got him though.

Everybody was laughing, even my Dad. I guess I was too. I was all covered with dirt and pine needles and fish blood.

"Damn," said the driver. "If we leave the fishing up to you, Ike, we're never going to fill the freezer."

He plucked the pole out of Ike's hands and dangled the line exactly in the same spot where Ike had gotten his strike. Sure enough, he got another hit.

"We should come here next year," said Ike.

The driver must have been a tuna fisherman in another life, or hungry, because he flipped that trout right out of the water without playing him for a second.

He boffed him dead on a rock and now we had two illegal trout in our possession.

"Ike don't eat much anymore," said the driver. "I'd like you to have the fish he caught, mister."

My Dad looked hard at the two fish. He'd never kept a trout from a catch-and-release area in his life. In fact he usually crimped the barbs off his flies when we fished this stretch.

"You go up to the road and look out for the ranger," he said to me.

There was nobody on the highway at all. The Park had opened only a few weeks before. I stood there a couple of minutes wiping the water and cold blood onto my jeans when that old brown grizzly bear of a car came out of the turnaround and passed me.

The driver didn't stop to say goodbye. He just drove slowly up the road waving his arm back and forth out the window at me without turning around. I waved back.

I walked to the river.

My father had already cleaned our fish.

"Put it down in the cooler under the worms," he told me. "We'll stop in Gardiner for the lemons."

Animal Rights
"Say It Isn't So, Cindy!"

> Only the mountain has lived long enough to listen
> objectively to the howl of the wolf.
> —Aldo Leopold

Those who oppose the animal rights movement should be shot.

I know the more hysterical among you may be bothered by the notion of People for the Ethical Treatment of Animals (henceforth PeTA) interrupting bass tournaments this summer by driving jet skis in front of the competitors, thrashing the surface of promising pools with bamboo to scare away the trout and, in general, enforcing their sunny new directive: "Fishing Is the Cruelest Type of Hunting." But I believe it is their First Amendment-protected, terroristic right to do so.

You see, the PeTA people have been cordial enough to mail to me a suite of pictures, which I happen to have arrayed in front of me upon my desk as I write this, and I am grateful. This morning, I am aroused by the possibilities of the human spirit. To be frank, I can hardly continue writing.

The model Christy Turlington, splayed out upon a bearskin rug without the bear, says, "I'd rather go naked than wear fur." And if Ms. Turlington should later decline to wear polyester, that's OK with me, too. Cindy Crawford cradles a cat, strategically placed. Patti Reagan Davis, the former president's daughter, cradles a small black dog, somewhere between be-Jesus and Beelzebub. Melissa Etheridge cradles Julie Cypher, and so on.

Now, I'm a gentle 6X-tippet kind of guy, but

these sorts of images make me want to go out and slit a wild boar's throat with a Swiss Army knife, run down grizzlies in the snow, club rabbits with clubs. Politics of the primal sort tend to get me all hotted up, I guess—a good thing if you happen to live in Montana and must rely on wood heat.

But what's going on here, really? It's a long way from fur to fish. I can sympathize with a model's personal decision not to wear fur, since synchilla is what a Texas mistress wears, those less-than-skin-deep girls from back home whose cheekbones weren't quite high enough and so had to make do. A New York model's worst fear.

But I've always considered Cindy Crawford and Kim Basinger (another PeTA pinup—order the poster on a cold winter's day) to be something like the sweethearts of the rodeo, the modern American media rodeo, that is, It-Girls and icons, like Betty Grable, Norma Jane Baker, and Lauren Bacall. Now it seems these PC *nudistas* are fronting for an organization whose slogan in regard to bronco busting is "Buck the Rodeo!"; in regard to sacred American holidays, "Thanksgiving Is Murder on Turkeys"; in respect to hunting; "Unfair Game." As for fishing, the PeTA people call it "Aquatic Agony."

Put down your cane pole, Jimmy Carter. Roll over Beethoven, Herbert Hoover. Hang up the hip waders, Dwight.

What's wrong with fishing?

Well, I always like to give the devil her due. Let's quote from PeTA's Wildlife #4 bulletin, "Fishing: Aquatic Agony" (available on your local Internet): "Fishes' lips and tongues can be compared to human hands in some ways; fishes use them to catch or gather food, build nests, and even hide their offspring from danger . . .

148

"The many species used for bait also suffer. In addition to worms (who, it is now known, produce endorphines, a physical response to pain), live clams, pieces of other fishes ('chum'), and live eels are also commonly used as bait, and chickens' necks and 'bull lips' (which are exactly that) are becoming increasingly popular in commercial fishing.

"Eating the flesh of fishes causes health problems for people. Like the flesh of other animals, it contains excessive amounts of protein, fat, and cholesterol, and can cause food allergies. Naturally occurring toxins (e.g., 'red tides') can even be fatal to humans . . .

"Given the suffering fishing inflicts, the health hazards to humans who eat fishes' flesh, and the heavy toll fishing exacts from all aquatic species and the environment, it makes sense not to fish, and not to eat fishes."

OK, weird use of language aside ("fishes' flesh," indeed), my first wife was a doctor, and she now runs a major American hospital. I don't want to get into that now. It has so little to do with dry flies. I'm just saying, in my life, I've read more than my share of the *New England Journal of Medicine.* Fish flesh is good for you. It may hurt them fishes' lips, but it will make you feel good, and you will live longer with cod between your canines and a bottle of Beaujolais beside your plate, too.

Wait, the PeTA people scream: "We are not built to be carnivores, we just acquired the habit of eating meat."

When did we just acquire this habit of eating meat? The first time the first woman saw the first squirrel, probably. Or maybe a little later, when a tasty mammoth waddled by, and a big rock happened to be handy.

I don't want to make excuses for humankind. The whole species is overevolved, if you ask me, screwier than a sow's tail, as Tex Ritter used to sing, and ready to fight at the drop of the first succulent caterpiller wafting down from the top of the triple canopy.

But the Finns and the Japanese eat a lot of "fishes' flesh," and they seem to benefit from it. Yes, there is polluted fishes' flesh on this planet, rock cod and *surubim* catfish whose gills have processed mercury and cyanide from mine sluices, tank farms, pesticide runoff, and—no kidding—the dumping of birth control pills into British streams, the estrogen load of which causes trout to skip their periods. However, it is not naked *boss* models who have missed Sunday school to clean up these rivers. It's chemists with fly rods in their hands, and confused trout boxers like you and me.

I wonder if, a few years down the baby-boomer pike, should Kim Basinger or Cindy Crawford score the role of Aunt Polly in the latest remake of *Tom & Huck,* will they cut out the crappie scenes?

From PeTA's own official history, modestly titled "Compassion in Action," comes this mission statement: "PeTA operates under the simple principle that animals are not ours to eat, wear, experiment on, or use for entertainment."

Well, I guess this leaves out Stupid Pet Tricks. As well it should. Late night television is smarmy enough (and let's applaud the saving of some good animals from some bad lab situations).

But to return to PeTA's position paper, "Aquatic Agony." *Bait are people, too.* Worms become sentient beings, since worms produce endorphines. Worms feel pain and so should not be dangled before the jaws of other sentient beings—fishes, for example. "Other animals you might find cowering inside a tackle box of terrors include frogs (now sold live in U.S. vending machines—just like sodas), mice (according to fishing lore one of the 'best' bassers in the States used live mice to lure the big ones), rabbits and roosters (artificial flies are often made from rabbit fur or the colorful neck feathers of specially bred roosters who are killed when only months old) and, of course, other fish."

Heaven forbid, shiners!

Didn't Patti Reagan's father flail for bluegills when once a farm boy in the Midwest? I believe he did.

As we read further in "For Cods' Sake!," an article in the spring 1997 edition of *Animal Times,* "The Magazine that Speaks Up for Animals," on the cover of which is a picture of Brigitte Bardot nuzzling a burro (author's note to himself: Please, can we just leave Miss Bardot out of this? Whatever political beliefs this great actress may have developed since filming the immortal *And God Created Women* should in no way diminish your own punctuated memories of hormonal underdevelopment), it says, quoting "For Cods' Sake" subheads here:

"They say . . . 'Without anglers, rivers and lakes would be nothing but open sewers.' We say . . . Right now, they're just anglers' trash cans. A study of one lake in Wales revealed that 64 percent of the litter left by visitors was found along the 18 percent of the shoreline predominantly used by anglers."

Stop. Couple days ago, I was nymphing the Gallatin River, and along Axtel Road I chanced to pick up a crushed Coors cardboard pack and a couple of Bud bottle caps, obviously left by Melissa Etheridge fans. In truth, I always pick up whatever litter may be left at streamside when I go fishing, because I feel this place is my place. I fish here, I live here. Chelsea Clinton is not going to clean up after me. I'm sure you feel the same way.

OK, let's stop right here *again*. What's this in the PeTA literature about the "States," the use of the abbreviation "U.S.," the reference to "Wales?" I know the Welsh once brought dog racing to Montana and that they were proficient hard-rock miners. I think Richard Burton was Welsh.

But what I detect here is a certain un-American incursion by these PeTA people, an organization, it turns out, that got its start in England, a land that long ago stripped itself of wilderness.

Ladies and gentlemen, we beat the British at Yorktown, but they have returned to steal our bass. And, obviously, they already possess our women. Cindy and Kim are being used.

I know the British are supposed to be our allies in the planetary competition against communalism and carp, but I think we can all agree as sentient beings that something went wrong—very much wrong—sometime between *The Compleat Angler* and *The English Patient.* It's often seemed to me that if American soldiers like my cousin Wreford, a naval academy lieutenant who ended up a San Diego admiral after taking out the first Japanese ship of World War II, the *Haro Maru,* had not put down their fly rods and joined the fray, the British would all be eating sauerkraut today, instead of, evidently, tofu.

We are the people of the Whiskey Rebellion. The British, by closing their Commons to yeoman hunters and anglers, lost their wilderness. Nobody with a stake in the wild was left to defend it. All that remains of wilderness in Britain today are some rose gardens and maybe a couple of dog obedience shows on the tellie.

I'm not saying the English are alien beings, or anything crazy like that. I'm just saying the American media is in danger of being seduced by Christy Turlington's buttocks.

We must get back to thwacking grouse with gun barrels, as the goddess Diana intended.

Just kidding.

Seriously, there is nothing environmental about the animal rights movement. Nobody who ever placed a terrier over their privates has yet managed to save a swatch of elk habitat. Nobody who scubaed beneath a Florida Keys bridge to chase off tarpon has ever lobbied for clean wetlands, bays, and streams in Washington, as fisher-folk do.

I've always been suspicious of Zen Buddhism, too. *Say it isn't so, Cindy!* All those little bonsai plants, so carefully arranged, twisted and stunted in their youth. It makes you want to order out for fish and chips, never mind the Rape of Nanking.

The silliness of vegetarianism is manifest, not because there's a problem with avoiding meat or fish. I don't care what anybody doesn't eat. That's their business. But to imagine that by striving not to shoot whitetail deer one is somehow living at peace with the earth is myopic at best.

"I now suspect that just as a deer herd lives in mortal fear of its wolves, so does a mountain live in mortal fear of its deer. And perhaps with better cause, for while a buck pulled down by wolves can be replaced in two or three years, a range pulled down by too many deer may fail of replacement in as many decades. . . . Only the mountain has lived long enough to listen objectively to the howl of the wolf," Aldo Leopold writes in *A Sand County Almanac*.

Leopold is a complicated writer, a hunter's poet, and in quoting him here I am condensing a bit, but what puts him up there with Thoreau and Li Po is that he sees the big sky. "Thinking Like a Mountain" is the title of this short chapter, which argues that if you shoot out the wolves, you will only create dust bowls, "and rivers washing the future into the sea."

I like wolves, but at this point I think you may honestly agree that the American wolf has been replaced by the American hunter. The mountain needs both.

I want to quote ranger Leopold one more time: "Too much safety seems to yield only danger in the long run. Perhaps this is behind Thoreau's dictum: In wildness is the salvation of the world. Perhaps this is the hidden meaning of the howl of the wolf, long known among mountains, but seldom perceived among men."

I can understand why somebody might not want to hunt. Hunting is a bloody sport. You track living things down. You kill them. Then you eat them.

"I shot a bird with a BB gun. It fell out of a tree at my feet. I don't remember if it was a crow, or what. And since it was wounded, my father made me kill it. He made me stomp on it with my foot until it was dead. I've never lost that memory."

This is not Aldo Leopold. It's Cleveland Amory, the father of the anti-hunting movement in this country and the president of the Fund for Animals. I called him up the other day as I was writing this, because it just seemed to me there was a confusing weird leap between opposing hunting and not eating the flesh of fishes. Also, I once had a conversation with Mr. Amory, long ago, when we were both opposed to the needless killing and abuse of dolphins, those carnivores of the open sea. I found Amory to be a gentleman, an American of the Old School, almost a true Montanan in fact—that is, somebody who calls it as they see it because that's the way they were raised and because, maybe, they guess that's the only way we'll all learn to see what's on the other side of the mountain, together, as Americans.

"Do you eat fish?" I asked him.

"Yes, I do," he said. "We are not against fishing. It's not a big thing with us. If I were a fish, I would want to be put back into the water. The Fund for Animals is not crazy about sport fishing, but to try to stop all fishing, well, too many people in too many countries would starve to death." Amory chuckled. "Now don't shoot any more of those buffalo out in Montana."

Cleveland Amory is old. He told me he would be turning 79 in a few months. I have a soft spot for old people. When they are not lying more, they tend to lie less.

The PeTA people are not about saving the wild. They're about spiritual arrogance. They have a fear of killing. A fear of eating. A fear of growing old and fat and, strangely, I suspect, for all their nakedness, a fear of sex.

I don't know why it is that fashion models make such bad actresses, but I think you need to be able to project at least the notion of a personality on the screen. This may not be quite right. Maybe they just eschew too much the flesh of fishes. Or they don't eat enough red meat. Katharine Hepburn hunted elephants, Lauren Bacall (elegant exception) was fancy with a Fenwick, and Brigitte Fonda—I think she uses Uzis on those gophers along the Yellowstone (though I'd have to check on that.)

I don't care about fur, because I never cottoned to women who wore sable. They were as arrogant in their own way as vegetarians. But I care about fishing, and it hurts me that America's mannequin queens should campaign for an organization that opposes fishing and hunting. It's British. It's elitist. I imagine Cindy Crawford sitting down to an endive salad in a Santa Monica cafe, and I think about a family of seven I know in Montana who put in for every doe deer tag they can get, and when they shoot an elk, they have a party, and we all go, and everybody's goofy and laughing while it's snowing outside, and during the replay of mom's hunt, cholesterol is not mentioned, and I can't help wondering if Cindy/Christy/Kim/Patti should not be condemned—to a sunny afternoon beside the Big Hole River.

There, a large, flat-screen television is to be erected, cabled to a VCR, solar-powered if possible, and it will play a continuous loop of *A River Runs through It*, until the sun sets, whence the Coleman lanterns are to be brought out and the bicoastals are to be handcuffed with daisy chains to the nearest willow and encouraged to read "A Treatyse of Fysskynge Wyth an Angle," penned in 1496 by Dame Juliana Berners, English nun, noblewoman, fierce angler, and early feminist—as part of *The Book of St. Albans*, thought to be the first book devoted to sport fishing and, in fact, one of the first printed books ever, a treatise in which, as I understand it, men are men and bait are bait.

When dawn shows her lion mane, we shall all have a line upon the water.

This is America, and in America it is always hard to call the millenium.

Fish on.

Do Fish Have Orgasms? (and if So, What Do They Sound Like?)

Do fish have orgasms? Recent advances in auditory technology have begun to answer this important question. Whether fish ask, "Was it good for you, too?" afterward has not, as of yet, been decided, but it seems the more vocal among the fishes practice simultaneous release (as, perhaps, should we) and that their newly discovered grunts, moans, clicks, and sighs may help humans to better understand the meaning of our own more refined and terrestrial gropings.

Trout in the clear blue streams of Wyoming, toadfish in the swirling murk off Sausalito, parrotfish on the coral reefs of the Big Island of Hawaii, hamlets in the Caribbean, and the brightly colored African cichlids of Lake Malawi, transported to home aquariums everywhere, all vocalize at the moment of completion.

Like the birds and the bees, the fish have their rituals. They select and reject with coos and protests. They wrap around each other like Madonna about a basketball player. Then, mouths agape, they cry out and release their gametes (or eggs and sperm, to the layperson).

Whooh.

How do we know this?

Because Phil Lobel has it all on videotape.

Phillip Lobel, a wry, bespectacled, and guilelessly erotic graduate of the University of Hawaii and Harvard, is associate professor of marine biology at Boston University's Woods Hole laboratory. He has taken three high-tech devices—the video camera, the laptop computer, and the hydrophone—and has put them together in something called, for better or worse, the Spawn-o-Meter.

Acoustic buoys have for some years been used by the Navy to track Russian submarines. The science of this was made popular in Tom Clancy's *Hunt for Red October.* Professor Lobel, who also happens to be the Department of Defense's chief scientist on Johnson Atoll in the Central Pacific, understood early on that the Pentagon was looking to put its expensive toys to peaceful use in the aftermath of the Cold War. At the same time, Lobel was bothered that the only way to scientifically study fish mating (which has implications for both pollution effects and commercial fisheries) was to net and capture the fish, cut them open, and examine their gonads. A highly invasive procedure, if you happen to be a tuna.

As much an engineer as a biologist, Lobel took a civilian prototype of the Spawn-o-Meter to Jamaica in 1989 and set up shop underwater, beside some love-smitten hamlets. The published results hit the scientific community like a tsunami. The seas were not so silent. "Do fish feel? Do fish have a language akin to birds? What are the implications for sashimi?"

Oblivious to the incredulous articles in *The Christian Science Monitor* and *Bioacoustics: The International Journal of Animal Sound and Its Recording,* the little hamlets burped, beeped, and pulsed away, keeping pretty much to high C, or about 256 megahertz, like Meg Ryan on a good night.

"I was amazed to find they produced a sound from within their bodies at that critical moment they were broadcasting their gametes," Lobel told me.

Professor Lobel and others then solved one of the enduring mysteries of San Francisco Bay by explaining that the somewhat unattractive midshipman fish, a close relative of the East Coast toadfish, was behind the weird foghorn bleats that annually spook houseboaters anchored off Sausalito. The male midshipman is simply calling to passing females from the nest he's built on the bottom of the harbor.

"Hel-loooah, Baaa-bee, I want your wad of eggs," says Professor Lobel, somewhat anthropomorphically imitating your typical toadfish in rut.

The lower the midshipman's voice, the more attractive he is to females (there's that midshipman movie with Richard Gere and a hippie girl at a factory, right?—*An Officer and a Gentleman*—and whenever Gere lowers his voice . . .). Anyway, Professor Lobel believes female midshipman fish are deciding who might make the best parent, since lower means bigger in the toadfish family—as in, the bigger the drum, the lower the sound—and if you're a female toadfish, you want, or maybe you have been genetically programmed to desire, the sperm of a dad fish big enough to guard your brood from crabs.

The toadfish and midshipman fish produce sounds by vibrating muscle against their air bladder, an internal balloon that keeps fish on an even keel and at the desired depth. Other fish stridulate, or move their fins in their sockets, which gives out a tantalizing creaky-door sound. Bicolor damselfish guard their territory with warning pops. Angelfish moan in recognition of each other. Sea horses snap "when exploring new situations." Jewelfish purr when they court.

But let's not get too deep too fast, here. At this point, there may be some justified confusion on the part of some listeners as to the basics of fish romance. While researching this column, I happened to be chatting with my friend Parks Reece, the wildlife artist in the above-water human laboratory we call the Murray Hotel Bar in Livingston, Montana, and Parks stopped me, in his North Carolina drawl, to protest that fish could not possibly emit orgasmic yowls, or even experience orgasm, because, by definition, *there is no penetration* among the fishes.

I was surprised at Parks's skepticism. Parks is not a lawyer, but a painter, and in fact, perhaps his most famous painting is titled "After the Spawn," a neomodern, swirlingly primitive work of passion that, nevertheless, accurately depicts two large German brown trout at the bottom of the Yellowstone River, each with a lit cigarette protruding from his or her conspicuously thin lips. "After the Spawn," indeed.

But Parks has a point. A fascinating one. When fish get it on, they vocalize by themselves, yet in close orgasmic proximity to their designated other. An untouchable reciprocal act of mutual masturbation. No wonder the toadfish live in San Francisco Bay. This is genetic magic. This is protected sex at its most primeval.

And yet it works.

Synchronicity maximizes fertilization. Write that on your bathroom mirror. We may eat them, but they have much to teach us. Why do trout, side by side on their streambed beds, scream (actually, kind of burp) at the same time as they release their—God, I hate that word!—gametes?

"I am not a mammalian physiologist," Professor Lobel tells me, "but part of the orgasmic purpose of vocalization and synchronicity in humans is to facilitate sperm transfer. Simultaneous secretions maximize the process." Vocalization makes the juices flow. Yes. And hi-de-ho. I mean, what is the purpose of rock 'n roll, anyway?

As you may already have guessed, Professor Lobel has a video out, called "Scrump," ("Life in the Fish Lane"), and it is in rotation on MTV.

"Scrump" starts out with Charles Agassiz, an even more legendary marine biologist than Lobel, falling head first into a tide pool. The video then proceeds, through damselfish squeaking, to parrotfish in a grouper grope. ("With the parrotfish/ Nobody knows," wails a tuneful blues singer, "Who scrumped who.") So far, this is all to the credible accompaniment of two extremely fetching female humans in halter tops doing the Auntie Mame thing, a kind of Barbados line dance. Then we get to Professor Lobel himself, in his office at the Woods Hole National Marine Laboratory, holding his patented Fish-Fone ($195, available from BioAcoustics, Inc., Woods Hole, MA) and rapping basso profundo, in an electronically altered voice: "Now the coral reef fish/Of the Caribbean sea/Have a mating behavior/That fascinates me/On a full moon night/They find a mate/Get together/And pro-cre-ate [cut to more images of fetching ichthyologists in halter tops]/If you listen real close/With the proper gear/Fish romance is what you'll hear—"

Kind of reminds me of John Lennon, when somebody asked him how he found America: "Easy, just turn right at Greenland." I mean, are the rest of us in the wrong job? You can have a Harvard Ph.D., work for the Department of Defense, and still make the rotation on MTV. Some people in our society are having too much fun. They're acting like fish and getting away with it.

All these new discoveries have implications beyond the merely titillating. For instance, Professor Lobel believes the noise from aquarium and fish hatchery pumps and filters may be driving many fish "frigging bonkers," and this is why fish "often cower at opposite ends of the tank" from noise sources. Fish are people, too.

Says Lobel, "Videos of fish mating, with the male dancing and the female cooing, turning gently on her side, make people more sensitive to fish. I'm a carnivore, myself. I used to do a lot of hunting. When my dad [Lobel grew up in the Midwest] was fishing, I would be looking around the shallows for catfish, mating. But I don't fish for fun anymore. I find it a little bit sadistic. The fish fights because he's not happy. When I fish for tuna, I fish to eat. I pull the tuna in and kill it quickly on the deck. Fish have fewer pain cells, but when they are on the end of the line, it's like the psychology of impending death, same as human prisoners of war. It's a form of torture. I don't care about lobsters, and I'm not a pacifist by any stretch of the imagination. When I'm in the field in Africa, I sleep with an AK-47 beside my sleeping bag, for snakes, poachers, or the errant mercenary. You don't screw around with me or my people. We'll defend ourselves. When I was in the Amazon in the late 1960s and early 1970s, it wasn't even illegal to kill Indians. This shocked me. My research was with the natives. But to fish for fun or macho-ness is no longer my mindset."

Lobel is one of those rare academics who, the longer he gently rants, the more you learn. He reminds me of Jack Horner, the Montana paleontologist, and also E. O. Wilson, the ant man, with whom I've chatted once or twice.

"In a way, we are all doing similar things with different animals," says Lobel. "We study how fish, dinosaurs, or ants evolved, but at the same time, how they interact with other species. What I have learned with sounds in fish is patterned after what Ed Wilson, whom I revere, did long ago with ants. Wilson showed how ants communicate. They read each other's chemical signals. They touch antennae and pass pheromones. But Wilson," laughs Lobel, "is light years beyond any of us."

That may be. But it is Lobel's nonacademic side, his almost innocent boldness, that has caused the real world to change, at least some small corners of it. During an expedition along the Congo River, in the Democratic Republic of the Congo, Lobel decided that the primate life away from the banks was so rich—the highest diversity and density of gorillas and chimpanzees in the world—that the territory deserved to be designated a national park. He brought conservationists from the United States and Europe together with the Congolese government. Poachers were turned into game rangers. Where the late Diane Fosse merely ranted, Lobel saved the megafauna.

"It is unproductive to parachute into Africa and tell local hunters, whose families are hungry, that they may no longer trap and kill chimpanzees or gorillas, just because we believe animals 'feel,'" says Lobel. "Poachers must be paid to change, if possible."

This article started out with an obscene premise, something about fish crying out in the depths, the seas no longer so silent. The work would appear to be taking a more sensitive tack. I'm not sure I'm comfortable with that. We are, after all, the animal that laughs. Like the hyena.

I ordered a Fish-Fone from Bioacoustics. It amused me to employ the same device Sean Connery and Alec Baldwin turfed with, at considerably more expense, though Lobel tells me my hydrophone is a shallow-water variety, which is part of why it costs only $195. I took my 6-year-old son Jack, and we drove out to the Bozeman Fish Technology Center. First, we lowered the Fish-Fone, which looks like a hockey puck on a cable, into a sluice tank full of hungry rainbow trout. There came an instant chorus of thunks on my bookshelf speakers. This turned out to be trout bumping the audio cable in their haste to swallow the food pellets Jack was raining down on them.

Then we tried the hydrophone on a herd of Arctic grayling, which, though in spawn, were shy, or so Dr. Dave Erdahl, of the United States Fish and Wildlife Service, told us. Then we dropped the Fish-Fone into a sluice with half a dozen albino rainbows and one 12-pound lunker German brown trout, known at the hatchery simply as "Mr. Big." Big rushed over and swallowed the Fish-Fone. Dr. Erdahl, Jack, and I went into momentary shock. Then Big spit out Professor Lobel's device and swam to the other end of the tank.

Jack and I retreated to Doolittle's Pet Shop in the Bozeman Mall. Here we kind of terrorized a $40 piranha, I think out of human revenge for what Mr. Big had done. The piranha seemed to think the Fish-Fone, with its disk "head" and cable "tail," was an anaconda. Then we relented and tried the device on Maxine—a 15-year-old, 10-pound, fruit-eating pacu, also from the Amazon—and then on some surly Malawian cichlids. But though we gathered a small crowd, we processed nary a peep. I realized writers probably don't have the patience to be scientists. Or else, as Lobel stresses, most fish are highly discreet about their moans, since they prefer not to advertise their position to predators.

Still, it seems to me, with the proper voice-activation device attached to the Fish-Fone, a fellow could have a pretty good time in the living room on a slow Friday night, eavesdropping upon the urges of neon tetras, until he realizes the smell in the kitchen is the rock cod burning. Fish have some-thing to teach us, but it's probably best not to lose our species identity over it.

Bottom line, I'm with W. C. Fields, when he shouted: "Water! Never touch the stuff! Fish scrump in it, don't they?"

Tackling Life

I have three good fly rods, a stiff big river Fenwick, a whippy little Cortland for the mountains, and an elegant custom job my brother made for me. But this is not as good as you might think, because the kids have broken them all, and though I have had them reglued, referruled, reconstituted, and repaired through the mail by the technicians at Robert's Wholesale Bait in Great Falls, Montana (a place so reasonable I hate to give out the 800 number), the Fenwick has already been mangled a second time, caught in the churning current of a closing overhead automatic garage door, and I have only myself to blame.

It was imprudent, possibly stupid, to have left the rod bungied to the roof rack, but I was reasonably sure I had pulled the Cruiser far enough inside the garage, until I heard the snap and twist of antique boron against suburban cedar, and I cast about for the remote to stop the door, sure I had left the clicker in a pile of old shoes or old magazines, and I just had it in my hands, when by that time any fool could tell the stick from Fenwick was only fit for UPS and Robert's, and so I howled then, as loudly as if my own thumb had been caught in the closing garage door, or the thumb of my older son who broke the Fenwick the first time, climbing onto the roof when he was smaller, because I love my boys even more than my fly rods, if that is possible.

But this does not explain what happened to the Cortland, the second time. That was my wife's fault, and I love my wife as much as I love my rods, perhaps even more so also, or how could I remain married to a woman so pathologically jealous?

We had been flailing the Madison at the top of

the Bear Trap, without extreme luck, and had driven up and around to Ennis Lake to see if they might be hitting close to the dam, when the boys yelled, "Let's go swimming!" and we had pulled onto the coarse black sand beach on the north side, where we became enthralled with the floating egg orange sunsets they have up that way, and a California woman, single with kids and a lot of dogs, golden labradors if I recall, had come over to talk, since talk is cheap at Ennis Lake, when the fish are not biting, and she had bent over to look for the mustard in her cooler—though my wife says she bent over because she was a slut—and in the process of her searching for the mustard, it became apparent—and I am not making this up as they say outside the sporting press—that her nipples had been pierced with trout flies, either #14 Royal Coachman, or Royal Wulffs of about the same size—I was trying to ascertain which, when my wife leapt up and fairly threw our kids into the same car whose roof rack would later eviscerate the Fenwick, and she started to drive off—without me.

"Wait!" I shouted, calmly.

I jumped in front of the car, which came to a jarring halt on the isolated dirt road. I ran to the driver's side, slipping the Cortland through the window without thinking too much—what I was really thinking about was how inanely commercial the sport of fly-fishing, or at least the lucrative paraphernalia business now so intimately connected to it, had become, so that some designer in Arkansas or Italy, or wherever they conceive these things, was actually manufacturing nipple ring jewelry in the shape of trout flies, and I climbed in beside my wife on the driver's seat, because she was in no condition to drive, having drunk a lot of beer from cheap aluminum cans, since we were so far into the Montana wilderness that bottles were unavailable, and the Cruiser began to coast toward the dam, somewhat unattended, with the kids in the back seat, shouting, and it was then that I managed to hear a sickening little crunch, which I instantly recognized to be the bite of steel door against delicate graphite, and I knew Robert's Wholesale Bait & Rod & Reel Repair in Great Falls would soon be receiving more of my business.

Sending your savaged blanks to Robert's is not the same as returning a guaranteed Henry's Fork Premium to the Orvis factory. I gather you take your chances on whatever is transpiring in Great Falls at the time of repair. The Fenwick came back fine. The Cortland was returned a little off-kilter, with a superannuated joint, a tick in the stick, like the limb of a white pine infested with weevils, the kind of bulbous burl they use in high-priced Western furniture now—or, to take us back to fishing, it looked like a hump-thwacked caddis covered with tiny pebbles and drowned orange pine needles crawling along the bottom of a cold shallow pool. I was not happy with the way the Cortland was returned—or, to abandon nymphs and dryads (all is language) and turn to a musicology simile, my rod was returned screwier than a sow's tale, as Tex Ritter once sang, in a nonangling context. Listen, for $5 a pop—yes, that is all the Robert's craftspeople have ever charged me for fixing anything—I am for pocketing all simile and getting back to the stream.

How do they fish, my three best, broken-fingered, lump-backed rods? They cast, they retrieve, the way Mark Twain's pool table played in Volume II of his unabridged autobiography, a book I recommend for getting you through the next two or three decades of your life with received grace. The felt was ripped on Twain's table. The slate was cracked. But the leather pockets held the balls just fine, and the game was all the more fun, given proper attitude by the players, which meant lots of silly stupid laughing, since life was as troubled then as it is now, and fishing equipment was probably no more safe.

The trout? In the face of my bruised arsenal? They don't know the difference. It's all in the wrist and tippet.

But what of the third rod, the one my brother made? It's a beautiful old thing, yellow fiberglass and walnut, from Herter's. My brother is dead now. Went down early. That is another story. And from repeated assaults and repairs, the rod, the upper half of it, has grown as thick as a British woman's calves. *(Don't stop me now, please.)* After the time I tripped while portaging a raspberry bush on the McCloud, the dog, back in the car, snapped my brother's creation like a biscuit. This was before I got onto the idea of roof racks and bungy cords, and before I ever had to deal with jealous garage doors, either. I loved that dog as much as—well, his name was Ed, Arctic Ed. A malamute, big fellow, 120 pounds after a meal of winter kill, clumsy but loyal, but mostly clumsy.

Sure, I could buy some clean new poles, from Walmart or Winston, but what is fishing all about, if not the stuff of memories, like the time about 1000 of us were dancing mostly naked from the waist up in an effort to Save Hapuna Beach, on the Big Island of Hawaii, from overrampant resort development. But this is another story, from another time, and it has nothing to do with fish, anyway, except perhaps reef fish, which are caught with nets, if they are caught at all.

Robert's Wholesale Bait & Rod & Reel Repair, 21 Eaton Avenue, Great Falls, Montana 59405; 800-553-2723; 406-454-1877.

Angler's Excuses

Water went over the top of my waders/Sun was in my eyes/Hackle came unwound/Bait was dead longer than I thought it was/Hooks were dull/Drag was set too tight/Handle fell off the reel back on the trail somewhere/Sight of the boat spooked him/Too hot, too bright, too cloudy/Pants full of chiggers/Tried to horse him in/Moon was full/Tippet broke, Knot slipped, Last year's tippet deteriorated–forgot to change it/Stepped in a hole/Otter ate the creel/Three otters pulled the steelhead under the water and when they came up they had chewed the fish gone/Grizzly bit the canoe/Barracuda bit the bonefish/Shark ate the tarpon/Tarpon yanked the outfit into the deep/Bullfrog grabbed the fly/Snapping turtle nailed the popper first/I fell out of the boat/Guide stood in my shadow/Guide knocked the fish off with the net/Eggs were not cured right, too warm, too rubbery, too old, freezer-burned/My partner got sloppy with the paddles/Fly-tyer put too much pressure on the barb–hairline crack/Seal ate the salmon/I broke the point off on the back cast/I was sitting on the wrong side of the boat/Bank was too steep to follow him/Guide pressured me/Should have used red/I thought it was the bottom/It didn't look the way it did on the video/Tied the fly on before I threaded the line through the guides/Left the reels on top of the car/Forgot my license/The boatman interdicted my hook with his forearm/I went out and jumped on the ice to make sure it was safe before I drove the truck onto it/The hole in the ice was too small/It was too sunny for a hatch/Guide didn't tell me the water would be this high/Too muddy, Too clear/Bear chased me into the bushes/Guide couldn't get me into fish/Fish got into the rapids/Fish found the stick/He broke me off in the weeds, nothing I could do/The graphite had a bubble in it–factory defect, I think/Boat was at the wrong angle /Hungover/ Sneezed/Shop sold me the wrong fly/Shop didn't sell me enough flies/All the feeding fish were on the other side of the lake/They don't call me Tannenbaum for nothing (I decorate the trees all year around)/The wind was in my face, The wind caught my line, Extracurricular wind knot weakened the leader, Chop concealed the strike/Swarms of mayflies and caddis harassed me so much I had to give up/Light was bad/The water temperature was too warm/Air cooled off last night/I stepped in the slack line and tripped/I lost my Prozac in the water and the fish started feeling too good to bite/I dropped the cellular phone overboard and the fish got more interested in stock quotes/They were all eaten by reintroduced wolves/I ran out of WD-40 for floatant and had to use insect repellant/There's just nothing but whitefish in this stretch/I was abducted and beaten by worm fishermen from Butte/Should have been here yesterday when they were really biting/While I was making an important personal emergency stop on shore, the trout, which were attached to the stringer, pulled my float tube into the middle of the lake/I released him 40 feet out/Fly was too big, too small, wrong color/Foul hooked him and the leverage snapped the line/Jerked it out of his mouth/The gods of pattern, color, and size all take second place to the god of presentation, and I guess I forgot to go to church on Sunday/Worm wouldn't wiggle/I don't keep score, My reflexes are slow, I can miss fish all day in a salmon-fly hatch, I don't even like to boat fish, I let him jump a couple of times to get a closer look, Fish must have been blind or slow/Fish suffered a concussion against the ice/Food, fishing, sex, it's all in the presentation/He didn't really take the bait, He only nosed it/It wasn't my fly he hit/I couldn't keep the fuse lit/I guess I just wasn't holding my mouth the right way/Fish struck too soon/It's always something.

With thanks to: George Anderson, Anonymous, Dan Bailey's, L. L. Bean, Jim Belsey, Al Bukowsky, The Fly Fisher Guide Service, Fly Fisher's Inn on the Missouri, Glen Gallentine, Capt. Warren L. Gorall, Nelson Ishiyama, Tim Johnson (R. J. Cain's), Greg Keillor, Mike Lawson, Bud Lilly, Gary McCutcheon, Charley McDonald, Judge Gregory P. Mohr, Richard Parks, Pirates' Cove Resort and Marina, The Powderhorn, Pat Roberts, David Schwartz, Tom Travis, Bob Ward's, Dave Williams, and Woody's Lures.

Bassing Disney World

A duck got caught in the jet engine. I think it was a duck. It may have been a goose. The FAA is not a precision instrument these days. Anyway, the flight from Montana to Disney World was a little delayed in Minneapolis. Then at 3 AM that night, the air conditioner at the Contemporary, which is an on-site Magic Kingdom hotel that's supposed to be real modern but was probably built as a set for a Pink Floyd concert, starts pounding and pounding. Next morning the lines at Splash Mountain remind me of Bulgaria, and I've never been to Eastern Europe.

So I'm licking my wounds poolside next to a large dancing hippopotamus wearing a pink tutu (the hippo, not me), when another Dad walks by carrying—strangely, under the circumstances, I note—a state-of-the-art bass outfit. He's also wearing a BassPro hat, got his 4-year-old girl by the hand. In the midst of all this Wonderland, he looks authentic.

"How's fishin', guy?"

"Awe-some!" He barks in a smokin' Carolina accent.

"Really?"

"Went out on one o' them Disney bass boats yesterday morning, and we caught 30 fish in 2 hours 'tween 2 and 10 pounds."

I'm supposed to be watching the kids in the pool, which is enormous, built next to the lake in the shape of a mouse's head with the ears being hot tubs, but what could go wrong? The pool's only 3 feet deep, even if it's an acre. I'm thinking, let's say this Southern fisherman and his little girl caught 20 fish in 3 hours, and the biggest was only 5 pounds. This would beat standing in line to get Cruella de Ville's autograph—which is supposed to be my fate tomorrow morning—by a whole heap of mouse burger.

 Dawn over the Magic Kingdom. *The orb of day rose as red as blood.* (This is not a quote from Donald.) Naturally, I'm a little skeptical, as our pontoon bass boat passes under the monorail.

We anchor off Cast Away Key, which is between the Polynesian Village and Epcot, in the middle of Seven Seas Lagoon. The monorail is to starboard, the Tower of Terror to lee, and my boys are wasting time feeding the fish.

That is, they are inserting shiners from the bait-well into the gullet of a 5-pound bass, which the 5-year-old just caught and the guide has consented to hold—quite calmly, under the circumstances—for pictures.

I gather it takes a special kind of guide to work the Seven Seas. Most of the anglers have the patience of 4-year-olds because they are 4-year-olds. Our guide, Jeff Gurshak, age 24, tells us that recent clients have included, nevertheless, adults who, after breakfasting upon beer, proceeded to eat all the shiners in the bait tank, as a sort of contest. Also, a woman who had never fished before catches a 4-pound bass. Then she catches a 6-pound bass. Couple minutes later, she catches a 7-pounder. This is getting in the way of her suntanning, so she reels in the line, puts up the rod, and gets back to her book.

I am struck illiterate by the ironies of the situation. It's like Kurtz said up the Congo, which I think

Michael Eisner has made part of Adventureland: "The ecstasy!"

This place is a 200-acre secret and God is allowing me, as an outdoors writer, to plug its hollows.

The record Seven Seas largemouth went 14 pounds, 6 ounces. There are now 90,000 largemouth bass in the Lagoon (and contiguous Bay Lake). Three years ago there were 65,000. There are also untold numbers of crappie, bluegill, mud fish, catfish, and gar. Gar? Probably a few 'gators, too. *(Note: A very few alligators, up to 5 feet, have been sighted.)* I bet they filmed *Peter Pan* in this bay. You remember the part where Captain Hook gets chased by the crocodile? What if one of my boys falls out of the boat? There will be hell to pay with the wife, back at the Contemporary.

But let's not get goofy here. Cinderella's Castle is straight ahead. we now have three fish on at the same time, and it is not yet 9 AM. A 5-year-old, an 8-year-old, and one coffee-fueled trout fisherman enjoying the type of largemouth bass fishing you're supposed to find only in Lake Okeechobee under a full moon.

The guide says the bass are entering spawning season. Maybe that's it. One of the boys asks why there's a splash next to a small duck swimming in and out of the reeds.

"Big bass," says Gurshak.

A to-scale paddlewheel steamer rocks our boat in its wake. It's plying the shipping lane between Ft. Wilderness and the dock at the Magic Kingdom. I ask if these big boats wreck the fishing. Gurshak says they make it better, by stirring up the bottom.

I get a lunker hit. Word is, a 3-year-old hooked an 8-pounder off the Ft. Wilderness dock last week.

Her father had to help her land it. But this boy feels bigger.

It only takes a minute to horse the bass in. As a Montanan, I feel a little strange using 15-pound test. Back home, we catch 6-, 7-pound brown trout on 14-ounce tippets. Heck, I've caught fish larger than that on the wife's dental floss. But this bass at the end of my line feels even bigger. This might beat the 3-year-old girl's record.

My wildest expectations are met. I'm thinking: next stop, the Internet. The fish is as long as Roland Martin's leg.

Graciously, guide Jeff Gurshak helps me heft the bass so that my son Jack may take its picture. You've got to let the kids cradle the Nikon sometimes. Don't criticize too much. Jack may be an Ansel Adams when he grows up. Don't want to discourage that.

Jack gets the shot.

Then he opens the camera. It's the 24th frame. My otherwise intelligent son thinks this means the end of the roll. He seems not to realize that this is a self-rewinding camera. I do not throw the child overboard. It is terrible not to have an official record of the event, but I think my word among anglers is good enough.

Anyway, we're out of film. We pull anchor and shoot over to the Ohana Gift Shop at the Polynesian. There's a stuffed marlin above the cash register, which is disconcerting, since we're catching bass in the American South—starts me to tripping about trolling for ahi off the Kona Coast—but never mind. Everything is disconcerting in Mickey's World. This is where the annual FINS tournament is held (*fins* is a play on *skins*, see, a tournament attended by both bassing and golfing pros).

We tool out to a different reef, Buddy Hackett Drop-Off, I believe it was called (Buddy was the seagull in *Little Mermaid*). Suddenly the fishing chills. The youth start to fidget. We don't hook anything for minutes.

Guide Gurshak tells us a little about himself. On weekends, he moonlights as a golf instructor.

"Really," I say. I have a friend, Rick Natkin, who wrote a fine movie, *The Boys of Company C*. Rick used to hate golf, I tell Jeff. Then, not so long ago, the Nat is examining himself in the mirror (early in the morning, even macho guys will do this, after a certain age), and he tells the mirror: "You know, I used to think golf was a game for fat, middle-aged, bald guys. Well, it's time to get out the clubs!"

Now Rick's a great golfer.

Jeff doesn't get the point of the story.

And there is a point, a very important one. I'm trying to catch the bass off guard. This is an old North Dakota trick. Fish strike when you least expect it, so you don't want to try too hard, in life as well as in fishing. "If it will, it will. If it won't, it won't." As Hank Williams's son sings.

The bass don't get it, either.

It's over.

We blast back for the dock at the Contemporary. I give the puzzled young Gurshak a $20 tip.

Forty bass in half an hour, I think it was.

My boys have no idea how good that is.

You never do, till you're 36 or maybe 38.

"Dad, Dad, Dad! Now can we go on the Star Wars ride?"

The youth are excited.

I'm thinking, OK, this place is as covered with gift shops as shingles on a leper, and what I'd really like, as an informed father, is a poster of Princess

Leia, one with the curled brass salamanders circling her Chattahoochees. This would be a vision for the Millennium.

"Sure, guys."

I mean, we be done bassin'.

Of Magpies & Marlin

KAILUA-KONA, HAWAII

As a people, we Americans tend to be eclectic in our stronger passions. In Washington it's politics and the President. In Los Angeles it's earthquakes, Heidi Fleiss, and O. J. In Texas there's always barbecue. But in Montana, where I'm from, what gets the juices flowing is the black-billed magpie, and out in Hawaii, where as a neotropical migrant I have wintered these last 20 years or so, the most heated conflict is over the state fish. Should it be that grand swordsman of the seas—the Pacific blue marlin—or, instead, a tough, territorial, testy, and not so tasty 9-inch denizen of local basaltic reefs known, hereabouts, as the humu, or more fully, the *humuhumunukunukuapua'a*, a name that is almost, but not quite, the longest word in the Hawaiian language?

These seemingly frivolous choices between totemic symbols carry more substance than we at first imagine, and they often tell more than a little about the changing ways we regard the environment.

But first, Montana and the magpie: that raucous, tuxedo-feathered member of the jay family, a bird that looks like nothing so much as a New Year's Eve reveler who can't stop partying and won't stop crowing about it.

Some people do not like magpies.

"I've seen cowboys—God!—stop the pickup, pull down a magpie nest, and stomp on the babies," says Roger Clawson, a columnist for Montana's largest newspaper. "This is not just vote-me-no-on-the-issue. If you're not out there smoking magpies with your shotgun, then you're considered slovenly, in some quarters."

"The magpie is not the kind of bird you want around the buildings," explains Dave McClure, the long-time president of the Montana Farm Bureau and a cattle rancher near Lewistown. "They make a mess. They scavenge roadkill deer. They rob the nests of the other birds. They will work a fresh brand or scab on cattle and sheep, and they have been known to peck the eyes from a newborn calf."

I have only talked to Dave McClure by phone, but I want to say that he sounded like a measured and reasonable man, to me, the sort of calm patriot who raises at a fair price what the rest of us are over-charged for in restaurants.

Still, Clawson is not exaggerating when he says that feelings against the elegant, carrion-snacking magpie run deep.

In the 1940s and '50s, most Montana counties paid a bounty of 10 to 15 cents for every pair of mag-pie legs turned in. It was believed killing magpies would save the eggs of game birds such as pheas-ants and grouse.

"We made enough money to go to the movies once in a while, sure," shrugs McClure, over the phone.

"It was really pretty neat," remembers Clawson, "'cause county clerks weren't ornithologists, and blackbirds were a lot easier to kill. Yet their legs all look pretty much the same, especially if you let 'em rot a little in a paper bag in the sun. Clerk give a quick look and take your word for it. You were getting your money's worth if you brought in real magpie legs. Magpies are bright. You can walk up in the middle of them with a pitchfork but you can't get within a 100 yards with a rifle. They seem to know the difference."

In fact, magpie eradication used to be practiced

throughout the West. As a boy in Unitah County, Utah, Jim Jensen, now executive director of the Montana Environmental Information Center, would hammer up 10 × 16-inch cedar "magpie boxes" to the trunks of cottonwoods. The boxes were stuffed with horse meat, and the horse meat was laced with arsenic.

"The idea was that the magpies would go back and feed their nestlings, but God knows how many eagles and hawks, mountain lions and bobcats were also killed. It was all part of our cultural antipathy toward the predator."

Five years ago, however, Jensen decided to do "penance." He had killed enough magpies in his youth, and he had grown up—born-again—to become the state's leading environmental lobbyist. Jensen proposed that the black-billed magpie become the Montana state bird.

He spun the issue with a bit of clever populism. Jensen railed that the reigning state bird, the otherwise loveable little western meadowlark, a mind-your-own-business songster that trilled "METHO-DIST PREA-CHER! METHO-DIST PREA-CHER!" (at least according to Montana's white pioneers) was not a True Montanan because it abandoned the state at first snowfall, like many wealthy summer residents, whereas the in-your-face magpie toughed out the state's notorious winters.

"The meadowlark right now reclines on a beach in the Bahamas, bedecked in sunglasses and Bermuda shorts and drinking a mint julep," said State Sen. Bill Yellowtail, who then represented the Crow Reservation and introduced Jensen's bill, in the month of February.

So what if the magpie indulged in a meal of flattened fauna on a slack day? We all have to eat.

Jensen and Yellowtail's campaign was meant to be educational, light-hearted. Their supporters rented tuxedos and bobbed about the legislative chambers in magpie top hats and tails. But for a week the state was stopped dead in its tracks, riveted to the debate as if it were the Clarence Thomas hearings. Editorial writers went ballistic, and this in a state that serves as repository for many of the nation's ICBMs. Yellowtail, whose ancestors were probably named for the red-tailed hawk, even began to receive hate mail. Before range war erupted, a compromise was necessary.

Senator Judy Jacobsen, a Democrat from Butte and no friend of the magpie, proposed that the meadowlark keep its crown but that the rival magpie be made "Official State Scavenger."

"I'd like to honor both of these birds in the way that they ought to be honored," she said.

The final vote on the scavenger amendment was 34–14, the magpies not having it. If this was a compromise it was a dirty one.

"I'm hurt," said Sen. Yellowtail, who went on to become the head of the Environmental Protection Agency for the Western Region, and, most recently, the losing Democratic candidate for Montana's lone congressional seat.

"I didn't understand the emotional depth of the opposition to the magpie," mused a bruised Jensen. "People say magpies peck out the eyes of newborn calves. That's true, but that's nature. Other Montanans are just as bad. We have a custom here of going out every fall and massacring harmless vegetarians and storing them in our freezers."

Clawson, who says he never brought in magpie legs for the bounty, though he may have been friends with some who did, even goes so far as to question the basic "Eye of the Newborn Calf

Charge," the heart of the ranchers' attack. "I don't think anyone's seen magpies pick brand scabs or a newborn's eye. That's just the ranchers' story and they're sticking to it. It's bullshit and you can tell 'em I said so. I do know magpies eat tons of mice."

"They said our bird sucked eggs," a bitter Janet Ellis, program director for the Montana Audubon Council, recalls. "They might peck an egg. But how can a bird suck? I admit," she admits, "that magpies will gang up on and torment house cats and rob them of their chow, but then I'm no fan of cats."

What are we to make of the magpie's defeat? Did the vote represent a primal human annoyance with creatures that dine on uncooked dead things? Was it, politically, the victory of Montana's powerful extractive industries over an imaginative but innocent environmental lobby? My own view is that we naturally select for emblems those animals that make us feel good about ourselves, and it is hard for the descendants of clean-living, hard-working pioneers to take kindly to a bird that dresses gaudy and flaunts sloth, its beak sometimes deep within roadkill. Makes no difference that the black-billed magpie is handsome. Beauty, in the West, is mostly nonutilitarian, the exception being horses and some humans. The drab meadowlark makes itself useful all day long by eating weed seed between rows of corn and rye, stopping rarely and then only briefly to digest and praise Methodism.

In the old days, that is before there were any white pioneers at all, the Crow Indians regarded the magpie as a bit of a trickster, and boys were called "magpies" if they happened to be mischievous and persistent, which to the life-loving, horse-stealing Crows, was not such a bad thing. Magpie boys, like the famous Chief Plenty-coups, might grow up to be strong, imaginative leaders.

Montanans are just now beginning to incorporate the spiritual and environmental traditions of native Americans. But they are still not ready to be represented by something so frivolous as a black-and-white jay.

Now, there are those in the island state of Hawaii, completely unaware of the magpie–meadowlark fracas, who nevertheless remember well the battle between the bald eagle and the turkey for the choice of this nation's national bird. In the islands, the epic battle over animal totems was played out not in the air but underwater, between the reef and the deep blue sea, in the official balloting for the Hawaiian state fish.

In the original debate, if you recall, Benjamin Franklin was vociferous in his support of the turkey, which he believed to be the all-American bird, defined in his mind as resourceful, far-sighted, and good eating. Other voices, perhaps wiser, perhaps not, cast their votes for the bald eagle, maintaining the warlike raptor represented strength and majesty and would add needed glamour to the image of a young nation, whereas the turkey was, well, a turkey.

But in Hawaii the eagle candidate, which was the blue marlin, a pelagic fish of legendary power and not coincidentally the favorite of the sport fishing industry, lost out to the *humuhumunukunukuapua'a*, whose name in Hawaiian means, briefly, "pig snout," or more fully, *fish with blocks of color and a snout like a pig's.*

To say something has the snout of a pig is not necessarily derogatory in Hawaii. The ancient Hawaiians liked pigs a lot. The pig is still the centerpiece of the luau, both sacred and tourist profane. And in truth, the humu's long nose is so graceful and sloping that it reminds me of certain classic automobiles, the 1937 Cord, for instance, or the 1949 Mercury coupe that James Dean favored. The humu's eyes are set so far back on its hood, or head, that they could probably look behind if need be, like a flounder's. The perfectly balanced ballistic nature of the humu body allows its tiny pectoral fins to turn it on a dime, and it has a shock of stubby bone for a dorsal fin that lets it wedge into holes in the coral should its dignified demeanor fail to dissuade predators. Its markings, those "blocks of color," are striking. The humu sports a blue lip mustache the shade of an island sky arching above its sharp crustacean-crunching teeth. Arrows of yellow enclose swatches of black and beige. A scythe of pumpkin orange curves below its eye, and all of this is etched and daubed above a belly as white as a lagoon moon. Not for nothing is the humu's *fauve* first cousin known as the Picasso triggerfish.

The beauties and charm of *Rhinecanthus rectangulus* were lost on marlin partisans such as Jim Rizzuto, associate editor of *Hawaiian Fishing News*. "The humu is a squat, fat, reef trigger fish that does nothing except piddle along and get into trouble," he huffs, sounding like a Montana meadowlark man.

"In choosing the humu, we chose a wimp to be our symbol," fumes Mark Suisa, a representative of Seagrant and the fishing lobby. "It was the frivolous choice of a frivolous society. The marlin gives us international stature, much as the awesome waves of the North Shore put Hawaii at the top of the surfing world. Yet the masses did not understand this."

It's true that my own vote was cast frivolously. I never expected to win, and I voted for the humu because I thought its name was the longest word in the

Hawaiian language. It turned out that another candidate, the long-nose butterfly fish, or *lau-wiliwili-nukunuku-'oi'oi*, has two more letters.

That nonresidents like me, as well as children, could vote at all may have made the campaign the most democratic in state history. "O-fish-al" (as I say, this was not an entirely serious contest) ballots were printed in most Hawaiian newspapers and handed out in schools.

In conception, however, critics came to view the election as rigged, since to qualify for the referendum a fish had to be "easily seen in its native state."

"We didn't want to include fish most people would only see dead, mounted, or on their dinner plates," explains Dr. Bruce Carlson, director of the Waikiki Aquarium, which helped to initiate the contest.

Obviously, a free-swimming 1000-pound marlin could not be put behind aquarium glass. Other pelagic dinner fishes such as the mahi-mahi, the ahi (yellowfin tuna), and the ono (wahoo) were also excluded. This was capricious and unfair, to hear Suisa and Rizzuto complain, as if men over 6 feet tall were suddenly not allowed to run for President.

Suisa and others crashed the aloha-shirt and black-tie political rally and dinner held at the Honolulu aquarium close to election day. Giant costumes had been made for the *humuhumunukunukuapua'a*, the *lau-wiliwili-nukunuku-'oi'oi*, the goat fish, the unicorn fish, the parrot fish, the convict tang, and the other, all reef, candidates. These tropical fish representations were marching in parades and at football games. Yet studies showed each excluded marlin brought to gaff (or environmentally tagged and released) during a fishing tournament was worth $43,000 in tourist dollars and assorted taxes. Just what was the economic worth of a *hu-*

muhumunukunukuapua'a? Probably not much more than a magpie's legs.

Ironically, though, the humu possessed million-dollar name recognition. The little fish was the star of the most famous Hawaiian song of all time: "My Little Grass Shack In Kealakekua, Hawaii." This *hapa-haole* ("half-foreign") chanty contains the line, "I want to go back to my little grass shack in Kealakekua, Hawaii/Where the *humuhumunuku-nukuapua'a* go swimming by." In Hawaii, "Grass Shack" is taught alongside the "Star-Spangled Banner" in schools and is also close to the hearts of tourists of condo-renting age, since it became the virtual theme song of the "Arthur Godfrey Show" on early network television.

So the goofy humu was not the underdog it at first seemed, and the marliners were not the mon-eyed backroom ranchers they initially appeared to be. The macho marlin could actually be seen as the hardworking salt of the sea, and the humu, just another magpie dilettante.

"We got the star of a flip contemporary song," says Suisa. "The humu has no biological significance. It came down to a distinction between what I call participants in the environment versus spectators of the environment. This translates to fishermen stewards versus those who want merely to look at fish."

This is an advanced distinction, and Suisa is automatically upping the environmentally correct ante by strutting it out. In Hawaii, those who were raised on fish they and their parents caught, and who fish for a living now, are not seen the way loggers and many miners have come to be seen by many in places like Montana. Hawaiian fishermen often re-gard themselves as native stewards of the sea, and those who "merely" want to look at fish are viewed as tourists.

Of course, the marlin industry has been one of the last blood sports in the world to see the environmental worth of tagging and releasing its catch, since tourists covet more than anything the Dead Fish Picture: a marlin harvested considerably before its time hanging by block and tackle between the angler, wearing a lei, on one side, and the Kona Coffee Queen, perhaps, on the other.

So the humu won in the streets, with a solid 16,577 of the 60,191 acceptable ballots cast. (One ballot deemed unacceptable was cast "in honor of our isle politicians" and was for the Blind Mullet.)

Nevertheless, one shoal remained. It was necessary for the legislature to certify the winner, and the legislators were not legally beholden to the popular vote. They were also much more sympathetic to the protesting partisans of the pelagic since those folks were adults and residents and cast real votes at election time. An awakened fishing lobby, like ranchers in Montana, did not want to be represented by a frivolous symbol. It might be bad for business.

It was all a little unreal. The Hawaiian fish fight was turning into the plot for a Frank Capra movie gone tropical.

The election was in danger of being overturned. Then sanity prevailed. A wise senator pointed out what harm such a move would do to the kids' view of democracy. The frivolous humu vote was allowed to stand.

I think tears were probably shed on the decks of twin-engine marlin boats from Honokohau Harbor to the Ala Wai Canal, and little sighs of relief were uttered in kindergartens from Kaua'i to the Big Island.

But that's America. In America, totemic choices can be serious passions, indeed.

Ted Turner's Backyard

Kathi Coyle, who had never shot anything in her life except targets, and those stationary and only the day before, unrolled the ice-fogged window of the big green Suburban and stared open-mouthed through the falling snow at the top of the Spanish Breaks on Ted Turner's ranch. Two hundred elk loped toward her, as if in slow motion, as if in a movie, as if, she could only think as she grabbed her borrowed .270 and jumped out, she had dropped back in time.

At 7245 feet, the Spanish Breaks are the second-highest point on the Flying D. They roll north off the Spanish Peaks in a hand of ginger: brown needle-and-thread grass, green juniper, steep close canyons of shadow and snow laced with raised veins of sparkling pink feldspar that take you by surprise like a jeweler's ring in the dirt. Finger ridges of volcanic andesite run further north off a main ridge until the breaks plummet to prairie and prairie meets river, the Madison on the side of the setting sun, and on the east, the Gallatin.

As the elk ran, clouds of powdered snow rose about their haunches like dust on a summer's day. The flakes floated through the faces of the cows. There was a mist of breath in front of the lead bull's mouth.

The herd charged down the nearest canyon, and Coyle slogged to get into position. She is a petite woman, about 5' 2", green eyes, dressed in wool that day. The snow touched her hips, in the holes.

Shots popped off to the west, in the direction of

the Madison, whipping the elk. Coyle dropped to one knee, fired point blank at the lead cow. There was a click. She had forgotten to put a round in the chamber.

Our kind have been hunting the Flying D since ice hunters speared woolly mammoths here, species of now-extinct horse, and, possibly, the evidence is not yet clear, tigers—sabertooths. This was a while back, 11,500 years ago, when folks were on their way down the eastern slope of the Rockies from Siberia to Tierra del Fuego, and still serious about spears. When bow-hunting was invented, 2000 years ago, the mammoths were already hunted out. Elk lived more on the plains then, but there were still plenty of bison and deer. Bones have been found in 200 sites on the ranch. They were killed by the Salish and then the Blackfeet, who drove the Salish north to Glacier, and the Crow, who held their own with the Blackfeet or anybody, trick-riding the new horses brought over by the Spanish and traded north, starting with the Comanche, through the land of the Utes, to southwestern Montana and the Spanish Breaks.

Paul Thompson, a dermatologist from Sequim, Washington, hunted the Breaks 2 years before Coyle. Fourth day out, the last day of his hunt, it was getting dark. Dr. Thompson was antsy. Searching for a Boone & Crockett animal, a record, or something close, he had passed on several trophy bulls. It was not real warm, below 20°, the temperature dropping with the light. The cold turned snowflakes to wizened pellets. At the end of one finger ridge, he and Flying D guide Jimmy Doran had glassed onto a good herd of 15 bulls and were in the middle of the stalk.

"It won't get nicer than that," whispered Doran, pointing to an animal with antlers like a crystal chandelier.

Thompson took aim, 325 yards with a .338, four-power Leupold.

"Don't shoot," said Doran.

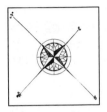 The herd smashed past Kathi Coyle. She shoved some bullets into her rifle, started back for the Suburban. Stopped. Halfway to a frozen-over creek a second herd thundered down the west ridge. Coyle cued and dropped her cow with the first shot. The animals scattered. Coyle, a church-going Catholic (except during the two weekend Sundays of the cow hunt on the Turner ranch), prayed she would not have to finish her animal with a second shot. She watched the elk slide down the draw, waited to see if it would move. She heard a clicking noise behind her. At that, she herself slid down into the snow, which in the bottom of the draw could be as high as her stomach. It was a third herd, so close she could hear the click of their hooves. She was downwind. She turned in stop-time, not to spook them. A brow tine was sniffing the air almost beside her. An old cow checked the wind with him. There were 30 of them. Shots rang out again, over the west ridge, on the Madison side of the ranch.

"I could hear them think," says Coyle.

They turned and ran into the junipers.

"Mine was dead as a doornail, shot between the third rib from the front, in the lung. I was dizzy with the beauty of it all."

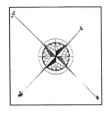

Dr. Thompson thought another hunter must have crossed onto the end of the ridge, into his line of fire, but Doran was pointing close. An animal with 8 curling antler points flying off both sides of his head had stepped out of some juniper 30 yards away.

Thompson killed his elk with a heart-lung shot. They dressed it by moonlight, placing the quarters on pine boughs, to be taken out next morning. The snow had stopped.

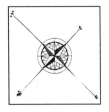

There are two types of elk hunts on the Flying D, the plebeian end-of-the-season cow shoot, like Kathi Coyle's, which several hundred specially licensed hunters participate in for free, and the regular season trophy bull hunts, such as the one Dr. Thompson gladly paid to enjoy, which now cost $9000. The Flying D covers 107,520 deeded acres, with another 30,000 leased from the Forest Service and the Bureau of Land Management. Soon after Ted Turner bought the spread in 1989 for $22 million, he put the ranch into a conservation easement under the auspices of the Nature Conservancy. This contract outlaws mining, logging, waste dumping, and the development of new buildings and most roads. The ranch can still be sold but it can be split into only a maximum of four pieces, while buyers or heirs must adhere to Turner's original conservation easement forever. In effect, Turner had made the Flying D into a game preserve in perpetuity. He set about removing 500 miles of fences and barbed wire, consolidated the old homestead structures, buried the power lines, began to repair stream banks, and replaced the cattle with buffalo.

"I just never liked cattle, even though my Dad had them," says Turner. "They trampled down all the grass, and that ruined the cover for quail, which I loved to hunt." He adds, "I intend to make twice as much from bison as you would make from cattle." Turner plans to mix business and solitude. "I bought the place to get away from people. Me, I want to live as far away as I can from everybody. I am becoming a hermit. There is nothing wrong with that."

Taking out the fences allows resident and migrating elk to roam freely in search of the best grass and forbs. This holds them on the property. The size of the elk herd has about doubled from 1800 to 4000 at last helicopter count. "Without the cattle," says Turner, "there will be enough grass left for them to eat."

Since the northern boundary fronts wheat farms, unsheltered plains, and the encroaching college town of Bozeman and the flanks are moated by rivers, the Flying D works as a funnelling honey trap for big game. To the south, a natural wildlife corridor runs all the way to Yellowstone Park, through the Spanish Peaks, Lee Metcalf Wilderness, and the Beaverhead and Gallatin National Forests.

"Turner does not own the elk," Jim Posewitz, author of *Beyond Fair Chase* and the former director of environmental affairs for the Montana Fish, Wildlife and Parks, once told me. "The people of Montana do. It was my job to drive up to the ranch and tell him. He took it well."

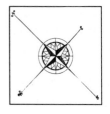

Beau Turner is not taking it well. First week of September, and he and outfitter Rob Arnaud are giving me a preseason tour of the ranch. In the near vertical scramble to the top of the Breaks, Turner's Toyota 4Runner has mired itself in dry dirt, the engine boiling over. Turner, 26, is 6′ 2″, cheerful and can-do. He is wearing faded blue jeans and a red cowboy shirt striped with black arrowheads. His father named him for Pierre Beauregard, the Confederate general who fired the first shot in the Civil War. He speaks with a light Georgia drawl. Arnaud, 39, is shorter, a tight, smiling cowboy in a white straw hat and sunglasses, fourth-generation Montanan from Livingston, with a degree in animal science. Arnaud used to run a wilderness pack and hunting business, but tiring of "nearly starving to death," he began to learn the art of elk management. His goal on the Flying D is to make elk and bison compatible on the same range. "Bison eat at the plate first," says Arnaud. "They are just not impressed with elk. I watched this 320 class bull elk try to move through the bison once. He displayed his rack of antlers, which always worked in his world, but the closest buffalo cow walked over and hooked him in the butt with her horns. That moved him."

We all get out to let the engine recover. It's as beautiful as any country in Montana, which is saying a lot. Down the slope on opening day a couple years ago, Turner took a sizeable elk with his bow:

> I watched for 15 minutes as these two bulls battled. They beat each other to smithereens. The cows were being pushed down the mountain. My bull lost and sidled onto a side trail,

close to where I was hidden behind some sage. He had some marks, some blood coming out. He was pretty whipped. Sometimes they go at it all night long. Each year, we pick up four or six heads, animals who die after goring each other. It's not for show. They go all the way. He was about 20 yards from me.

The 4Runner consented to continue. We reached the top of the ridge. Leaning against the cairn of a Salish vision quest, Turner and Arnaud explained the mechanics of elk lust:

Basically, the bigger bulls win out the bigger harems. But if you see bulls with 30 to 50 cows, you know you're having some problems with your bull-to-cow ratio. On public lands, they have 10 bulls or less for every 100 cows. Those cows have to go out and find bulls to breed them, and they might miss one, two, even three heat cycles. Or breed to a lesser bull. An unproven sire. Then the survivability of the calves goes down because they're born later in the year, with less of a chance to make it through the winter. Those older bulls have also worked themselves to death, cleaning up the cows.

They talked of one herd of 1400, which later broke up. As the eerie sound of bugling elk ricocheted off ridge and canyon, this sea of ungulates turfed and mated, dominated by old bulls in the center constantly challenged by young 6 × 6s, while out on the unprotected edges spikes darted about trying to jump the occasional meandering cow, "like teenage boys," as Arnaud phrased it. (Or as Mark

Twain once put it, "There are no wild animals until we make them so.")

It made me think of a passage from Byron W. Dalrymple's *North American Game Animals,* a book that should be known to every boy who learned to read before he learned to shoot. Turner and Arnaud seemed just a little dry in their statistical rendition, but Dalrymple is, well, America's poet of rut: "Wild-eyed, nose running, caked sometimes with dripping mud, [a mature bull in full rut] urinates and ejaculates on its own hocks and belly, and screams defiance until the mountains ring."

I did not share my literary memories. We bumped down the west side of the Spanish Breaks to the bunkhouse.

"To call it a bunkhouse is to use the term loosely," recalls pay hunter Larry McGovern. "Accommodations were as good as my own bedroom and I live well. The food was better, and you can print that so long as my wife doesn't read it."

McGovern killed a 7 × 7 his first day out, with a Dale Goens .300 Winchester using 180 grain Federal. He hung around for 4 more days, "eating multiple rack of lamb."

The bunkhouse to me seemed homey enough, stone fireplace, cedar paneling, log walls, wildlife art. "Bring your dirty underwear and your rifle," shrugged Beau, stretching out his hands.

"I'm not trying to promote the ranch," says Chuck Swinehart, who raises harness racing horses and has hunted the Flying D 3 years running.

But I've hunted Africa. I've hunted the West. Some guides can be lazy about finding you big bulls. Some can be crude people. Some might take a look at you, and because you're putting on some years and are from Ohio, they might hike ahead of you and look back with condescension. That's not the way it is on the Flying D. Turner's guides all get along. A hunter gets a personal type of situation. They'll work to find you a big bull. It's a free chase camp. The elk are not behind some enclosure. They have the habitat and they put you on it. You know you're not there just to make someone else money. It's a conservation effort beneficial to the elk.

The drill is this: Upon arriving at the ranch, a hunter immediately sights in his rifle, through a hole in a warm cabin, under the eye of Arnaud. If a shooter can whack a tick off an elk's ear at 300 yards, fine. If he can't, fine, too, but noted. Guide and hunter will stalk close.

"Some camps assume the baggage handlers have done a good job, but you don't want to wound an elk of this size, simply because your scope got bumped," says Dr. Thompson. "Next they give you a little slide show: 'This is a spike, please don't shoot. This is a rag horn, please don't shoot. This is a 5 × 5. Don't shoot. This is a small-tine 6 × 6. Try not to get excited.'"

After lunch that first day, you go hunting. The ranch is divided into five guide areas. Each hunter gets 20,000 to 30,000 acres to himself, four to five hunters at a time over the entire spread, only 30 hunters a year. (When Dr. Thompson thought another shooter could have been in his line of fire, he was theoretically mistaken.) Hunts are usually "spot and stalk." A fine animal might be spotted in the first day or two, but it might take 2 or 3 more days to put the elk in a hunter's sights.

"Time works against you by the hour on the Spanish Breaks," says Marty Wood. "The thermals rise in the morning, but fall in the afternoon as the temperature drops. You can almost feel your scent dropping with the wind."

Turner, Arnaud, and I wound round the Madison end of the ranch. Here, the Turners are spending $80,000 to control leafy spurge. There, they are catting up a stream bank to restore the mud mush left by decades of cow tromping, putting back the meanders, stocking effluvial grayling, which are endangered in Montana. In a couple of areas where management doesn't want the game to go, there were fences with an electric strand powered by little solar converters. We pound up a ravine. "Ted," as the owner is referred to, had decided a dam would be nice here, and so guys were wailing away against the hillside with steam shovels that would cost more than many Montana ranches. We're approaching "Ted and Jane's" house.

Before we arrive, we crest a ridge. Below is a sight that floats my heart: 3000 free-ranging buffalo.

"I got up at 5:30," says Arnaud, "and by 10, when I headed to work, they were all gone, all 3000, over the range. By tonight, they might all be back. Very mobile."

Beau Turner ticked off some of the advantages of buffalo over beef: They get sick less, require fewer injections, no hormones. The cholesterol in a buffalo steak is much lower than in beef.

"Cattle just don't make sense," Ted Turner says. "We imported them from Europe to begin with, but they don't really work. It's just hard to change." He adds, "With cattle, you've got to plow and sow and fertilize and irrigate and reap and bale and store it and build fences to keep other wildlife from eating what you baled and stored and then you have to feed all winter and start all over again in the spring. That's expensive." Turner once boldly told a crowd of cattle ranchers in Bozeman, "Unlike cattle, bison don't just eat the best grass. They'll eat the weeds and plants. Unlike cattle, bison don't need hay in winter, except for the buffalo calves." Buffalo will "scrape down through the snow to get food. Their metabolism slows and they require less forage. Their thicker coats better insulate them. They don't ruin rivers and stream banks like cattle. They don't wreck tree stands. They stick to the plains, grazing in the fiercest sun, not sheltering in shade. And they're cleaner. They wipe their bums."

Such talk met with resistance, if not disbelief, when Mr. Turner first moved to Montana. "For Turner to tell us how to ranch," said Malcolm Story, the legendary 90-year-old grandson of the very legendary rancher who drove the first Texas longhorns to Montana, "I find that entertaining, and I don't think I'm alone in saying that."

"My father didn't feel Turner knew enough to comment," Pete Story, also a bit of a legend in southwestern Montana, told me this summer. He laughed. "We don't want a war of words with a man who owns a news network. My dad had no malice. Buffalo meat is leaner, but the buffalo is a dangerous, unpredictable animal. They go where they want to go, unless you're wealthy enough to put up the big fences. We had a dozen, until Luther, the big bull, took his horns, opened the stockyard, and led the herd onto the highway."

"Cattle are bred to be stupid, lazy, and fat," says Ted Turner. "Anything that lazy gets fat. I have nothing against cattle ranchers. I just don't like cows."

For lunch, Beau, Arnaud, and I stopped off-ranch at the Kountry Korner Cafe. We had chocolate malts and buffalo burgers, the red meat of the future. I paid. The buffalo tasted, to me, somewhere between fresh white-tail doe and moose, chewier than beef cow and also gamier, in a nice way, very filling though, for all that little hit of cholesterol.

Ted Turner plans to reintroduce America to the preferred meat of our pioneer ancestors, and the locals they displaced, in about 1998 and in a big way. The Ted has no incremental ideas.

"Prime cuts already go for about $16 a pound at Harrison-Teeter's in Atlanta," said Beau. "I've told Dad, the secondary cuts might work as hot dogs at the Braves games." (Ted Turner owns the Atlanta Braves.)

"These elk cost a lot of money to keep on the ranch," Arnaud mused. "If Ted so desired, he could run 5000 bison and cut down the amount of elk."

Of course, the annual end-of-the-season cow hunt is designed to do just that, cull the herd. Such magnanimity divides locals. "The cow hunt helps Turner's image a bit," grouses an owner of a local sporting goods store, "but there's too many bulls up there. They're breaking their antlers. Also, letting the coyotes grow cuts down on the deer." Some other hunters believe that excellent conditions on the Flying D prevent prime bulls from wandering onto the nearby public forests where they can be shot.

I called Gary Wolfe, executive vice president of the Rocky Mountain Elk Foundation, in Missoula. Wolfe received a Ph.D. in the population dynamics of elk herds, managed the Vermejo Park big game ranch for 12 years, and had hunted the Flying D twice."Moving the buffalo from pasture to pasture has resulted in better grass and better forage," he said. "The elk are fat with good bodies and sleek coats. I believe there are more trophy bulls coming off the Flying D than off other ranches. True, you have a higher ratio of bulls to cows than on the forest service, but in places like Yellowstone Park, regulated by nature, there is also a higher bull-to-cow ratio than there is on heavily hunted public lands. As for coyotes, I haven't seen any in three trips."

There are coyotes on the Flying D, as well as a few hundred sheep. Turner keeps the sheep to eat the leafy spurge. He believes if the coyotes dine on a few sheep, that's balance. In fact, he'd very much like to have some Rocky Mountain gray wolves, such as the ones reintroduced to nearby Yellowstone Park. "I'd especially like it if they culled some of the elk," he says. "Of course, it would be another story if they bothered my bison. I sound like a cattle rancher, don't I?"

"It is the trophy hunter who provides the habitat," said Beau. Beau Turner talked of traveling to Botswana to hunt. "Half that country is a hunting preserve. I'm not talking 100,000 acres. I'm talking half a country. But if you fly along the border of the land where the cattle and other animals are allowed to graze, that strip is a complete desert."

A few minutes later, Turner launched into an explanation of why the bobwhite quail was doing OK in the South. The love of sportsmen and women for "that one little bird you couldn't hit with a wing shot" has protected "the only ancient mixed forest left in the Southeast." Farmers and landowners will forgo spraying pesticides on their crops, risking their living, "because they know pesticides demolish quail eggs."

Young Turner started a diatribe against the Sierra Club—"To Hell with the Sierra Club!"—because they had, in his opinion, sold Montana and the Rocky Mountain states downriver by refusing, on a national level, to support the Northern Rockies Ecosystem Protection Act, which would have preserved vast corridors of wilderness for elk and elk hunters, hikers, and anglers, along the lines of the Alaska wilderness bills several decades ago.

After lunch, we toured Turner's house, an unpretentious four- or five-bedroom log home overlooking the Spanish Peaks and an artificial trout pond ("mostly dinks," shrugged Beau). The father is a demon fly-fisherman: "I find it to be my second most favorite thing to do, but a reasonably close second." He and Jane Fonda used to attend Trout Unlimited meetings at the local Holiday Inn.

It is a very comfortable home, a black lab and a golden retriever, if I recall, guarding the two-4 × 4 garage. The furniture is old-style western leather. Action movies are piled on the VCR. The only signs of elegance are the formal dining room, with a long table that might have seated 12, and Albert Bierstadt's painting of the Wind River Range over the fireplace.

"Dad asked me to get that for him. I think it's probably worth more than the house. Nobody in the media has ever been here," says Beau, with a bit of unintentional irony.

At the end of a long line of trophies is a regular buffalo head of a whitetail deer bagged by Beau as his father attempted to wrest the rifle out of Beau's hands.

It was the end of the season. Beau was younger. Ted Turner had decided to go hunting, though he had the flu. He was walking back toward a ranch road, head down. He had left his gun in his truck, scouting. Beau and Arnaud came driving down the road, and just then this enormous whitetail burst in front of them all, and froze.

Beau Turner leaped out of his truck and loaded his rifle.

"Oh, no! Oh, no!" shouted Turner, Sr., running back to the road. Ted Turner grabbed hold of his son's gun but Beau clenched his teeth and wouldn't let go.

Turner threw up his hands. The deer made the mistake of watching father and son struggle. Beau shot the whitetail.

"I am an unlucky son of a bitch," said Ted Turner, slumping into his truck.

"I gave him the head," shrugged Beau.

There are about 700 whitetail deer on the ranch, and perhaps 800 to 1200 mule deer. Only 5 to 20 are killed in a season. They can be large. In 1994, Marty Wood took the largest mule deer shot in Montana in modern times. Each year a contingent of hunters is willing to front the full elk fee simply to get a shot at a trophy deer, for an additional charge of $3500. Some people like to put in for buffalo as well, a sort of three-for-one romp through the old and new West. The buffalo hunters often use black-powder rifles. A dozen or so bison are shot each year.

The Flying D is a working fantasy. It makes sense that an out-of-state communications mogul would be the one to understand, instantly, what the ranch had been all along: a state-of-the-art leap into the frontier past. Take out the cattle fences, and you have something better than *Bonanza* or *Lonesome Dove*. You have the way it once was, Lewis and Clark, the Blackfeet and the Crow, the big sky in the palm of your hand. You have the way our spaceship-launching civilization wishes they might see it, if only for 4½ days of serious hunting.

Now or Never for
American Rivers

If you sink the back of your hand into the sphagnum moss below a granite boulder at the top of Henderson Mountain, 2 miles northeast of Yellowstone Park, your palm will fill with water so clear it is as if nothing is there, water so cold your fingers will hurt. This is good water to drink. This is water trout like, too, and there are plenty of them, rainbows and browns, down the mountain, where this trickle becomes the Clark's Fork, and soon enough the Yellowstone River, the longest undammed stream below Alaska, a river Michael Keaton is trying mightily to protect as he rips off his sport coat while standing on top of a banquet table in front of Al Gore and 1000 river and fishing conservationists at the annual American Rivers celebration in Washington, DC.

Even the Vice President laughs.

"I thought Al was pretty loose," remembers Keaton. "He wants to laugh but you've got to get him there. I say to these environmentalists: Lighten up—but persist."

Never much identified with causes, Keaton, a Midwestern bait-caster transplanted to the fly-fishing waters of Montana, is persistent, and passionate, about saving the Yellowstone and the Clark's Fork. For 2 years he has been spokesman and a director for American Rivers, a small, sinewy organization of 19,000 members with a powerful board of directors and a bipartisan win–win style of solving problems. American Rivers is perhaps best known for its annual list of North America's most endangered and threatened rivers.

"Let's not hand over one of our most precious wild places to some mining company that just wants to make a quick buck, and leave the rest of us with a time bomb, a disaster just waiting to happen," says Keaton. "We have to draw the line."

Acid waste could churn the granite-clear waters of the Clark's Fork into a Gatorade orange, the color of too many of the streams Keaton grew up near in the strip mine country of Pennsylvania and West Virginia.

"The first time I ever saw a clear stream, I was about 16, out with my dad and my brother, and I just couldn't believe it. It was so beautiful. You could see all the way to the bottom, and there were trout darting about. A singular event for me."

"Today," says Thomas J. Cassidy, general counsel for American Rivers, "if you want to go out with your kid and catch what you caught with your dad, well, a lot of those fish ain't there anymore, like the West Slope cutthroat, bull trout, Idaho or Atlantic salmon. Or if they are, there are far fewer of them. More than a third of North America's fish species have become extinct or rare. Aquatic resources are crashing, and this has brought about a confluence, so to speak, between fishing groups and river groups."

American Rivers's former chairman Ray Culter cites "The National Water Quality Inventory: Report to Congress," a 1992 study only recently released, which states that about 40% of the nation's rivers and lakes are already too polluted for fishing, swimming, and boating. The bottom line is if you want to catch fish, you've got to have clean water, and if you want clean water, you must save rivers.

"It ain't rocket science how you save a river," laughs Cassidy, a bearded man of short Falstaffian proportions.

We are standing beside Hyalite Creek in south-western Montana, two valleys west of the Noranda mine site above the Clark's Fork. Cassidy has a Black Dog ale in one hand and my fly rod in the other.

"What do I do now?" he asks. Cassidy is an angler of perhaps more enthusiasm than experience. He also has a fish at the end of his line.

"Could drop the beer and take up the slack," I say.

Cassidy prudently nestles the bottle between two rocks.

"Yes! He's still there!"

"About saving rivers, Tom—"

"It ain't rocket science," Cassidy begins again, his smile as big as the captured rainbow is not. "Number 1: Protect the headwaters, which usually run through public or Forest Service land. Fight to have them designated 'wild and scenic,' as the Clark's Fork now is. At the least, make sure their banks cannot be logged. A bank without trees or cover silts the river, and fish cannot spawn. Number 2: Protect the riparian areas downstream. Meanders, setbacks, and marshy areas filter pollutants from subdivisions, septic tanks, golf courses, farms, and factories. Number 3: Appropriate flow. Dams kill rivers. Flooding brings nutrients to young trees and fingerlings, triggers spawning. Dams that are likely to be here to stay must, nevertheless, provide enough water downstream. No water, or channelized water, means fewer fish, different fish, or no fish. This is why the Yellowstone is not the Missouri."

American Rivers helped to win a Supreme Court decision allowing states the power to set appropriate instream flow requirements when they certify federally licensed dams on rivers inside their borders. American Rivers has long had a strong record of helping local groups to protect such famous wild rivers as the Kings, Tuolumne, Klamath, Colorado,

South Platte, Tatshenshini, and Clavey, all of which were on the endangered list at one time.

Stopping the building of what would have been one of the largest open-pit copper mines in North America, the ill-conceived Windy-Craggy project near the Tatshenshini and Alsek Rivers in Alaska and British Columbia, not only saved great numbers of trout and king salmon but also resulted in the preservation of a wilderness larger than Yellowstone Park. When combined with the contiguous areas of Kluane National Park in Canada, Wrangell–St. Elias National Park, Glacier Bay National Park and Preserve, and part of the Tongass National Forest in the United States, the Tatshenshi–Alsek watershed now makes up the largest internationally protected wilderness on earth, some 23 million acres, which is a lot of water for the great-grandkids to flail with red daredevils (barbs pinched). As of last December, the Tat and surrounding areas have been designated a World Heritage Site, just like the Galapagos Islands.

American Rivers's "Most Endangered List" is a sensible Hollywood gimmick that works because it gives television and the nation's op-ed pages the bait they are most like to rise to: simplicity.

Designating the Colorado River number 1 in 1991 drew trenchant questions and cameras to a nasty secret. The Bureau of Reclamation was washing out beaches and banks with unnecessary release surges from its Glen Canyon Dam. Public pressure resulted in the Grand Canyon Protection Act of 1992. Listing the South Platte as number 1 in 1988 and 1989 helped to save that blue ribbon trout stream from the Denver Water Board and its planned Two Forks Dam.

It's not that we don't need electricity or that dams are bad, believes American Rivers. It is that some big dam projects have taken on a life independent from the actual needs of consumers, who can, these days, often acquire their water and especially their energy more cheaply and efficiently from other sources such as natural gas or do more with less through elemental conservation on the one hand and new high-tech methods on the other.

Making the list elevated California's Clavey River to national prominence. The 47-mile long Clavey is considered to be the only intact aquatic ecosystem left in the Sierra, holding rainbow trout genetically unchanged since Spanish times. The rushing river was designated one of the first California Wild Trout Streams in 1971. But for the past 10 years the cement pall of a hydropower scheme has hung over the Clavey's plunging canyon. Developers wanted to build a 400-foot dam and suck 19 miles of the river through a giant pipe, which would eliminate 99% of its flow, not to mention most of its fish.

"We used to get hard looks and caustic comments from the local Wise Users," says Joe Dailey of the Tuolome River Preservation Trust, "but the list alerted national politicians and the media that the river was worth saving and that we weren't some fringe enviro or fishing group squeaking out there in California."

Prospective industrial customers took a hard second look at the inflated cost of the proposed hydroelectricity, and home rate payers began to howl that they would be the ones to pay for the dam's construction. Last February, the dam scheme was tabled, though not killed. Hydropower projects are like vampires, and only God can create a dam site.

"The Clavey's a fly-fisherman's paradise, mostly white water and pools," says Don Moyer, former regional manager of California Trout. "A good angler can catch 50 fish a day on it." He recommends a big #8 Wooly Worm on top, with a yellow or brown Wooly as a dropper fly, a foot or so below.

One of the likable things about American Rivers is their insistence that salmon could certainly be restored to the Kennebec, or the Penobscot, or the Columbia/Snake ("Where 16 million fish once spawned, only 300,000 wild salmon and about 2 million hatchery-raised remain,"says the List). if we as anglers and voters did the right thing by the fish. Twelve years ago, I was in Stockholm, Sweden, gawking one afternoon not at the usual tourist cathedrals, but at a half dozen fishermen standing below the city's central bridge. At the foot of sky-scrapers and beside a busy, honking boulevard, they were catching 20-pound salmon.

Imagine, if you will, pulling on waders at lunchtime and wandering down to the Hudson in New York, the Charles in Boston, the Chattahoochee in Atlanta and hooking fish the way Native Americans and early white settlers did. And—further caveat—that the tasty flesh of these salmon, sturgeon, trout, striped bass, and perch would not be so full of mercury and cancers that we would endanger our own health by barbecuing them.

One showcase urban river that would be fun to fish would be the Anacostia, a ribbon of slime that rides ever high on the most endangered list. The Anacostia flows, or rather, glurks, along within walking distance (and an elevator ride) of the Oval Office in downtown Washington. Clipper ships used to drop anchor in the Anacostia. Now canoes falter in its mud, fish suffocate in its silt, and on summer nights little icebergs of sewage offer the redolence of a medieval cistern. This ugly duckling of a stream is undrinkable and should not be swum in, but, remarkably, there are still brave crappies, bass, and minnows who ply its murk.

As part of its Urban Rivers Program, American Rivers persuaded the Environmental Protection Agency to post warnings to anglers not to eat these fish, and I suppose it is no accident that only the city's poor would think to drop a line. But now American Rivers is moving to clean up the mighty Anacostia, and Washington's congresswoman Eleanor Holmes Norton has introduced a bill that would help grassroots groups, anglers, and neighborhoods take back it and other rivers of faded glory across the country.

"I have never fly-fished the Anacostia," says Bob Bennett, who happens to be President Clinton's personal lawyer, and a director of American Rivers. "But wouldn't it be wonderful if we could? As an organization, American Rivers is not about fly-fishing Western rivers—yes, the directors do, and my soul gets touched and my brain cleared by doing so—but clean and fishable rivers are for the health and enjoyment of everybody."

Bennett has a 5-pound, 2-ounce German brown trout mounted at eye level beside his office door. Underneath, a brass plaque reads, "If I had kept my mouth shut, I wouldn't be here." This much is reported from time to time in the nonfishing journals. But I wanted to know where Bennett caught the brown.

"In the Missouri, in Montana," he replied, which would almost make it official business, since at least the lower Missouri is on American Rivers' list. Since 1943, dams and the Army Corps of Engineers have turned the 732-mile lower Missouri into a shipping channel, at great cost and little return to the taxpayers.

"What sort of fly were you using?" I asked.

"I thought I had hooked bottom, and then the bottom started moving," said Bennett.

He wasn't answering the question. "Nymph or dry?" I pressed.

There was a pause on the part of the President's lawyer.

"I'm taking the Fifth on the fly. I don't want to hurt the feelings of purists. I might be drummed out of the organization. Let's just say it was in my younger days."

At Bennett's first board meeting, he was from time to time interrupted by phone calls from President Clinton, presumably of a nonriverine nature, since Bennett was counseling the President in the Gennifer Flowers affair. One of the minor bits of board business was whether to allow a men's cologne company to use the American Rivers logo of a flowing stream in exchange for a $50,000 contribution. It seemed like a good idea to most, but Bennett, off the phone, interjected: "I don't want to be too outspoken at my first meeting, but what are we going to get involved in next, the marketing of condoms?"

A few days later, Tom Cassidy paid a visit to Bennett's office.

"Bob," he said, as he looked back at the gasping trout, "I did want to let you know the staff has taken to heart your suggestion about marketing condoms in the name of American Rivers, Inc., and we already have a slogan: *The only reservoir you'll ever need.* "

Bennett, naturally, was very strong against the Noranda mine at the headwaters of the Yellowstone.

"Look at this from a commonsense point of view," he says. "You're taking probably the strongest ecosystem in the world and subjecting it to incredible risks, in perpetuity, and for what? The idea that a Canadian company like Noranda can buy our land for $5 an acre, under the antiquated 1872 Mining Act, and put in peril a national treasure like the Yellowstone and Yellowstone Park—well, I believe the American people would knock down their congressmen's doors if they knew. This is not about the right of business to make a profit. This is about endangering our system, our health, our rivers, and our fish—in return for negligible profits by people who if they hadn't bought in so cheap would have no profits at all. It's like Will Rogers said, 'You can't make land anymore.' Well, you can't make rivers anymore, either, so we better protect what we've got."

When President Clinton eventually visited Montana, he told a Billings audience, "No amount of gain that could come from [the mine] could possibly offset any permanent damage to Yellowstone."

Following American Rivers's bipartisan style, the suit by the organization against the carpet-bagging Canadians (tied to the Bronfman family, long-time owners of Seagrams scotch and LaBlatte beer—what terrible sacrfices will campfire drinkers be called upon to make should a boycott ever be called?) is being carried by attorney Donald Ayer, the former number 2 official in the Bush Justice Department and a deputy solicitor general under Ronald Reagan. Ayer is a partner in the world's third-largest law firm, Jones, Day, Reavis & Pogue.

"If we can't prevent this type of mine in this place, then our ability as a civilization to make rational choices is in doubt," says Ayer.

It is probably well that the leadership of American Rivers seems to be about one part populist Democrat, one part rock-ribbed Republican, and one part those who would rather be fishing, since it could be argued that the nation's rivers have become the unintentional victim of a political drive-by shooting. Congressional elections have bestowed great power upon resource Republicans such as Rep. Don Young, and Sens. Ted Stevens and Frank Murkowski, all of Alaska.

"Will the Alaskans now block the Forest Service from protecting stream buffers from intensive timber harvest along the Thorne and other rivers?" asks Cassidy. These are prime runs for steelhead and salmon on Prince of Wales Island, in the Tongass National Forest.

But why conclude on a base political note? There is a sublime saying that has great currency around the American Rivers office: Two-thirds of the human body is made up of river water. This has sporting implications.

"It's pretty simple, actually," says Michael Keaton. "Water comes out of the ground, off the mountains. It goes into the cities, into a glass, into your body. It's just so taken for granted, yet it's a finite resource."

The Yellowstone
The Lodge Where All Dance

Underneath the Pine Creek Bridge over the Yellowstone this fine spring morning, ice cakes chug along like lily pads in search of a party. The Yellowstone may be the watery soul of Montana, joining mountain to prairie, but this day the watery soul is slushy, at best. It is coolish, standing in the middle of the Pine Creek Bridge in Paradise Valley. I don't mean to say cold. The temperature has been above 15° since dawn, and also, I'm wearing sunglasses. Full sun over paradise, those parts of the valley where it is not snowing, of course. Springtime in Montana. In the black pellucid water below, a whitefish is feeding between green granite rocks. On the bank, an antelope munches rabbit-brush standing next to three black-baldie crossed cows. Perhaps the antelope is being cordial. Perhaps she is only seeking warmth among the domesticated.

The hardy poetic side of me says what I should do is de-bungy the kayak from the roof of the Trooper, jump on the river, and write about it. But we Montanans have grown soft some time during the last century, I think.

Plenty-coups, who used to lunch with my Great-Uncle Charlie when Plenty-coups brought his five wives to Billings, once talked of how in the old days a teacher would toss a handful of peeled sticks into the winter Yellowstone, calling out, "Go get them, magpies!" and the young "magpies" would instantly strip off their shirts and leggings. "There was no waiting, no shirking. In we plunged amid the floating ice." The boy who brought back the most sticks might count coup. "The ice taught us to take care of our bodies," said Plenty-coups, who would become chief of the Crows. "Cold toughens a man."

Indeed it does, but still I wait and shirk. Cold also hurts, especially if one should suddenly find oneself upside down, trapped if not wedged, beneath still ice, inside a cheerful red touring kayak that will not roll due to operator turgidity. I think only an Aleut could execute an Eskimo roll today.

On the west side of the bridge, near the entrance to the Mile High Hereford Ranch, I can read a home-made sign: "Wishing Wells Made to Order." Such a sign holds many possibilities. But this is a practical moment. I wish for warmth.

It is time for a retreat to the tributaries.

An hour later and 50 miles up Highway 89 from Pine Creek, steam rises off the Gardner hot pots. The pots, formed by the raucous meeting of the icy Gardner with the boiling runoff from Mammoth Hot springs, lie near the Continental Divide. Careful where you spit. They'll drink it in San Francisco over your left shoulder, Manhattan (New York) over your right. Across the tumultuous little Gardner, elk graze the hillside. On my side of the stream, Jasper, the Samoyed, is pouncing upon the voles of spring, crashing through the crusty snow that still covers their mouse tunnels. Under the steam, I am naked, warm, flushed, and mostly submerged, the skin pinkish and cooked orange as a brook trout's belly. The droplets on my beard only freeze if I stick my face in the wind for more than a minute or so. Under such tropical conditions, a philosophical mood is easy to sustain.

About 4 miles downstream, the Gardner tumbles into the Yellowstone as brashly as a baby with a saxophone between its knees. This is where the big river begins for those who want to float, paddle, or swim it, legally. Officially, I suppose, the Yellowstone gets its start as a rivulet of Wyoming sweat rolling off Yount's Peak south of Yellowstone Lake, the largest body of high-altitude water on the continent. After a placid wallow through the Hayden Valley, the river buffalo-jumps 109 feet over Upper Falls, 308 feet down Lower Falls, and fairly screams inside Black and Grand Canyons to the confluence of the Gardner at the edge of Yellowstone Park.

The Yellowstone is a gorgeous piece of wetness, spring, summer, winter, or fall, the longest free-flowing river left in the Lower 48. A couple of years ago, in a family float, we—myself, my Brazilian wife, and two savage toddlers ages 3 and 1—went the distance, 671 miles (minus those 80 currently illegal—and probably pretty unrunnable—ones inside the Park) to the confluence of the Missouri River, in extreme eastern Montana.

It was a biblical journey, at least for me. That is, it was like falling in love with four sisters one after the other.

First comes the Upper Yellowstone, a mountain girl, thin, fast, rocky, always innocent, deep in spots, and a little crazy. She's stronger than you are. Take care under a full moon. The Yellowstone through Yankee Jim Canyon instilled the most fear in me, and there's hardly time to be afraid, in Yankee Jim. The canyon's black walls flash by quickly. But after 20 minutes of spray and blessed-equilibrium-shouting, the river smoothes out under the delicate wrought iron of Tom Miner Bridge, the entrance to Paradise Valley.

Now you bed a fuller bride, with greener eyes, though equally sassy: an older sister of a middle river. She gives you an elbow, this broader Yellowstone, looping you around the mountains, the Absarokas and the Beartooths, rather than ripping you straight through the peaks pell-mell, the way her blue-eyed upriver younger sister did. Paradise Valley is a slide of alfalfa and granite. I always spend as much time looking up—at Mt. Delano, Mt. Cowan, the notch through Mill Creek, the shock of Himalayan grandeur that is Emigrant Peak—as I do paddling the eddies in front of me. It is a distracting stretch, this middle river from Carbella to Laurel. Sometimes it is easier to dump in the unexpected and occasional white-water slurry of what used to be called the Great Bend than it is to tip in the concentrated sluice of Yankee Jim.

Between Laurel and Billings, the Clark's Fork joins up. The first feeder stream with muscle, it adds 9.6% of the Yellowstone's total downstream volume. In 1806, William Clark named his tributary "The Lodge Where All Dance," believing this is what the Indians called it. Clark rightly thought that was a funny name for a river. But there's a beauty to the phrase "The Lodge Where All Dance." I like to think of the Yellowstone itself as "The Lodge Where All Dance." Sometimes I even like to think of Montana that way.

At Billings the Yellowstone turns briefly into a working girl, Western Sugar, TK Sulphur, Montana Power's Corrette coal-burning plant, the Conoco refinery, Exxon, middle fingers of lipstick flame jamming the black night air below Sacrifice Cliff with natural gas odor. Strangely, from the river, this urban stretch is still plenty wild. The turn at the Billings KOA is a bow-thumper. Cottonwoods mostly wall off trailer courts and the Norwest skyscraper alike. (Twenty stories and you can scrape some sky, in Montana.) Not a mile below where the sickly sweet effluent of the Billings sewage treatment plant dumps in, a foamy white, three deer jumped in front of my boat, until they were swept back to shore by the current, big eyes screwy with panic.

Finally comes the Prairie River. She's a farm girl at first, raw boned, big bodied, slow to rile, except during spring rise, when her cottonwood sweepers sometimes tumble end over end like Ferris wheels. A watery rodeo for the foolhardy. A strong woman, this prehistoric sister of a river, the oldest of the four, you do what she says. Being a modern guy, maybe you kind of enjoy that, wandering down those braided meanders until it's so shallow the carp rest their scaly bellies on the bottom and suck down mayflies with pink mouths that won't close till you whack them with your paddle. Disgusting! Time to portage.

This purposeful prairie river from Billings to Miles City slowly becomes rangier and rangier as it enters *makoshika*, the badlands, below Terry. At Terry, a place as rangy as Montana gets, the Powder marches into the Yellowstone like a ghost cavalry. This is a good place to camp for a long time. Sitting Bull and his people wintered here in 1868. Supplies for the ever-gay George Armstrong Custer were off-loaded by steamship at the confluence of the Powder, in 1876, and the dead bodies of Custer and his officers were onloaded a little while later, nearby.

You stretch out, space out, on the lower river, losing yourself in vistas of beige rock, parallel lines, your own breathing, until suddenly around an oxbow above Glendive, a 40-gondola train loaded with Colstrip low-sulphur thunders onto what you thought was an extinct Milwaukee and Chicago Bridge. This part of Montana used to be the bottom of a vast sea that stretched from the Arctic to the Gulf of Mexico. Since the late Cretaceous, *Triceratops* and *T. rexes* have languished in the layers of dried mud, like pressed flowers. Some homesteaders went around the bend in the badlands of the lower river, counting the howls of the wolves under a twisted yellow moon as the stock became caught in the brushy bottom. Evelyn Cameron, the now famous British photographer who ranched here at the turn of the century, languished but refused to go mad. Her pictures display order, care, the gathering of a landscape and a life.

But I like to think, having paddled through this sunken escarpment of the mind that is the deep prairie Yellowstone, that what our prehistoric lizard sister of a lower river would truly like to do is pull off her cotton dress in the middle of the sod cabin floor and press you against her bed of willows, the way it used to be done and is no longer allowed to be remembered.

Now that New York and Santa Monica have taken over the mismanagement of the Montana myth, what's missing, what's been expurgated, is what a guilelessly sensual place Montana was, and is. So long as you own a good down bag, of course.

But enough of river gal imagery. Drown me in beer at Madam Bulldog's Bucket of Blood, an offriver joint Calamity Jane used to shoot up when it was owned by Kitty O'Leary, a century before it became the Livingston Bar & Grill. Missoula's Jeannette Rankin was this country's first congresswoman, after all, seated alone for 20 years. Montana women were respected even before they were allowed to join the National Rifle Association.

It's funny where the mind wanders when you paddle a river as long as the Yellowstone. In the mountains, you focus on fish—the German brown, supercilious Bavarian import, hard to catch; the innocent black-spotted cutthroat, Montana born and bred, and a little bit gullible for it; and that oft-derogated prince of survivors, the mountain white fish. A Montanan always keeps a hook in the water.

Below Billings, I liked to set a trot-line of road-kill rabbit and restaurant T-bone for channel cats. Below Miles City, I trolled Rapellas behind a kayak, searching for the wily walleye and the salty sauger. At Intake, I pitched a red-and-white daredevil into schools of golden eye. A true Montanan eats them all, perhaps drawing the line at carp. Perhaps not. Even golden eye are quite tasty, fried in butter and shallots. The trick is to use a small nutting fork to pick the meat out between the rows of endless bones. I haven't yet joined the rush to impale giant paddlefish at Intake, sweet as their flesh may be. It's a question of morality, and deep ecology, as well as a matter of owning ocean tackle. How would *you* like to be snagged with a 4-inch treble hook while in the throws of mating?

By the middle Yellowstone, birds hold sway. Fish swim away. The memory of an osprey lifting a trout below Duck Creek Bridge stays with me. That day was so cold the drops of water falling from the airborne fish froze before they rejoined the river. A ruffled kingfisher waiting in the shade of Pompey's Pillar, a great blue heron stabbing the shallows near Shepherd, geese above Glendive flying off the river as the kayak approached, dozens, sometimes hundreds of them, surprised, honking in gravelly crescendo, shocked to see a human in a red boat.

Birds fly away. Trees stay. A forest is a forest on the sides of Yankee Jim, but downriver, single trees stand out, and they are always cottonwoods, wild, turning color as if they had feathers, the lazy, willy-nilly monsters of the bottom land.

What does the Yellowstone mean to Montanans? Before the railroad, the river was our E-ticket ride back to the "U-States," as Clark referred to civilization. A little later, in the 1970s, the river almost became a coal slurry to power blowdryers in Chicago, moving Montana coal in a great big water pipe. But good sense, I think, put a stop to that. Montanans have always taken care of their river, preserved instream flow, stopped towns from dumping untreated sewage, yanked out the car bodies that used to riprap the repository curves (though a rusted '52 International Harvester, twisted by Spring Rise and carved by side snow, probably deserves a lighted corner in the Yellowstone County Art Museum).

The Yellowstone has come to mean a lot to Montana. Whether you are jump-shooting ducks near Savage or feeding them in Sacajawea Park, in Livingston, that flow is like blood in the body.

I recently read a statement defining what in California is called ecopsychology: "Ecopsychology holds that there is a sympathetic bond between our species and the planet that is every bit as tenacious as the sexual and aggressive instincts Freud found in the depths of the psyche."

As aggressive and sexual as most of us neoprimitives like to think we are, this is still the sort of statement a Montanan has to read twice to realize: Not everybody in America has a Yellowstone running through their backyard.

A little while back, Tom McGuane wrote that a river like the Missouri ought to go through south central Los Angeles. It might have a calming affect. (At least you'd have to shoot across 50 yards of water to hit the other guy.) The same can be said of the Yellowstone, which, unlike the Missouri, nobody got around to damming.

Be glad *La Roche Jaune* flows, especially if you live somewhere near it.

They say Montana is changing. But I say, so long

as German tourists in the Gardner (tributary) hot pots refuse to wear bathing suits in flagrant disregard for federal regulations, and no rangers happen by, there is still probably hope for the frontier way of life. Since inclement weather has a way of grinding down even the most cheerful, Montana is always in need of spiritual uplift, because it takes the chill off. Until certain religious groups moved here from more desertlike climes to scotch our homespun morals, I don't think anybody white in Montana believed in God unless the winter was—*cold.*

A hundred years ago, the Episcopalian Church was probably the warmest place to be in Montana.

In the spring.

ACTIVIST OP-ED:
WHAT IS A RIVER WORTH?

Montana's Yellowstone is the longest undammed river left in the lower United States. It is a national treasure tumbling out of our first national park in a blue cascade until it joins the Missouri River 671 miles downstream.

But the Yellowstone River is about to be placed in danger. Noranda Minerals, a Canadian company, through its partner, Crown Butte Resources, is planning to start construction on a huge gold mine 2½ miles from the northeast entrance to Yellowstone Park. Set high in Montana's spectacular Beartooth Mountains, the New World Mine will sit near the source of three of the Yellowstone's most famous feeder streams, Soda Butte Creek, the Stillwater River, and the Clark's Fork. To catch the poisonous runoff from the mine, Noranda plans to build a 90-foot dam to create a tailings pond the size of 69 football fields. An estimated $800 million worth of minerals lies in this pristine alpine location 2½ miles from the northeast entrance to Yellowstone Park.

The mine is worth a lot of money; its reserves of gold as well as silver and copper are worth an estimated $800 million. Yet, as the director of resource management for the park said, "I guess if you threw a dart in a map of the United States, and decided to put a gold mine there, it's probably the worst place possible—high elevation, next to Yellowstone, grizzly bear habitat, three drainages. It's just a bad deal all around."

Although Crown Butte has revised its plans in response to environmentalists' complaints, the fact is that the tailings pond will always present a risk in this fragile setting. If it is damaged by avalanche, earthquake, or erosion of the pond's plastic and volcanic clay subsurface, acid waste could flow into the Clark's Fork.

If the mine is expanded, the waste could flow into Soda Butte Creek and the Stillwater as well. If any of its feeder streams are polluted, the mighty Yellowstone itself—since water has a stubborn habit of flowing downhill—could be harmed for generations.

A section of Soda Butte Creek has already been poisoned by mining pollution from the last century. When I was growing up, a friend and I attempted to fish the creek, flailing the water for hours with Royal Coachman dry flies, then Wooly Worm nymphs. In desperation, we switched to impaled grasshoppers. Nothing worked. Soda Butte, that stretch at least, had become a lifeless sluice. It has not recovered.

This must not happen to any part of the Yellowstone, a great and historical river. At the end of the Lewis and Clark expedition, in 1806, the explorer

William Clark floated back to "the U-States" by way of the Yellowstone's muddy rapids.

An example of the dangers facing our great rivers occurred in Colorado's San Juan Mountains last year when a mining disaster poisoned the headwaters of the Rio Grande. Caused in part by leaching from a tailings pond, it was the costliest mine pollution accident in Colorado history. The company responsible went bankrupt, and the Environmental Protection Agency says the cleanup could end up costing the taxpayers $20 million.

Whatever the risk posed by the New World Mine, a paradox is that because of eccentricities in the 1872 Mining Act, Noranda, like all mining companies, has been able to acquire government lands at nineteenth-century prices and need not pay royalties on the minerals extracted.

Large-scale mining—improperly sited—is not the only danger the Yellowstone faces. Pesticide and fertilizer runoff also affect the river ecology. When Gen. George Crook bivouacked near the lower Yellowstone, during the time of Col. George Custer's defeat, his troops caught thousands of cutthroat trout a week. Today, trout in the lower river are gone because of the impact of human habitation.

Perhaps they should be "restored," to use the environmental term. Perhaps it is also time to designate the Yellowstone River a "National River" or a "Wild and Scenic River" with the special protections such status affords. The twenty-fifth anniversary of the Wild and Scenic Rivers Act comes in a few weeks. What better way to celebrate it? Perhaps it is time to agree that any threat to this most special of rivers is too great.

Along the Yellowstone, we must not trade trout for gold.

Confessions of an Eco-Redneck

Author's note: In the summer of 1996, the scheme to expand the Canadian-owned Noranda New World Mine was tabled in a federal trade-out for as yet undetermined public lands in (presumably) less sensitive areas. The pressure came from grass-roots groups, the Greater Yellowstone Coalition, American Rivers, environmental lawyers in Washington, a Pulitzer prize-winning series of editorials in the *New York Times*, thoughtful broadsides in *Sports Afield* and the outdoors press, a couple of visionary congressmen such as Pat Williams and Max Baucus, and a few million or so eco-rednecks, fishing fools and burnt-pine-hugging Yellowstone Park visitors, who vote.

Marriage, Guns, & Pheasants

Last day of bird season in southwestern Montana, the Brazilian and I, desperate, finally find time to go pheasant hunting, something I haven't done since I was a boy, and she, never, though not a bad shot at the Ipanema Hunt Club, where they still use live pigeons, offering them up in sacrificial handfuls to a tropical sky. I would have liked to have known her then, under whatever flimsy shooting vests they employed in that terrible humidity.

Married now. Two children. No sleep. We practice with plastic milk gallons half full of frozen water. I lob them in a flowing arc above the cracked ice of the creek behind the house, and she attempts the slaughter wearing gloves. Cartons win, for the most part. Sky less than tropical.

Accessing private land proves the next problem. Gentlemen rancher friends, the kind of people who send photo Christmas cards of themselves sitting upon dead caribou with a .300 Weatherby ("This year we shot Rudolph") are already full up, better friends having descended for last week of season. We decide just to get out there, knock on farmhouse doors.

Kids dropped off at on-demand day care. Whoa! Pheasants everywhere. Hunter hysteria increases. Who owns this parcel?

Precious hours of daylight wasted chatting with historical invalid ranchers, guys in barns manufacturing airplane fuselages, at-home drunks. Modern farm life—though these grousing Walter Matthaus are almost as much fun to meet as real grouse.

Old man comes to door, preceded very slowly by aluminum walker. Black plastic cat-clock waggles away the seconds behind him. Cyclops of modernity glows with soap opera from the living room. Old man so cordial I am dead from waiting. His huge green eyes are younger than all of us. He points over my head. Stuffed pheasant in full flight mounted above transom.

"Fellow like you shot him," old man says. "Beaucoup birds on my land. Coffee?"

The Brazilian, honking the horn as she tries to turn the heater up, smiles from the driveway at her rudeness.

"'Course, if everybody could come here and hunt, the birds wouldn't be as thick as they are," says the old man, who, it turns out, has the same last name as the main street in town. "We want to make it better for fellows like you. So we won't be allowing hunting till next year."

Well, this is understandable. I suppose.

Next farmhouse turns out to be a factory. Dairy barn holds half a dozen small fixed-wing aircraft. Manager in white lab coat excited to meet the Brazilian. *"Muitos, muitos aves,"* he smiles. Tons of birds. His mother was Brazilian. Montana, land of snow and samba. Outside, the sun begins its tremulous descent over the glaciers. The man throws a hand up at the big windows.

"Unfortunately, I only lease the property. Did you know a Brazilian invented the airplane. Yes? The Wright Brothers were cough drops."

Ha-ha.

It used to be different. My father and I would drive out in the green '57 Chevy from Billings, east along the Yellowstone, past Huntley to Hysham, a stack of Sunday papers and a box of apples between us on the front seat, all that was necessary to garner permission. Of course, these isolated folks never had any guests. My father on these rambles would be wearing a white shirt and a tie under a canvas hunting coat so authentic, the blood stains were browner than the olive eyes of the rancher's oldest daughter. This was not about hunting. This was about Sunday morning, about Montana, about catching up on the news. Now they have home delivery of the morning paper. Think of that. Now the state flower is the satellite dish. Well, can't shoot birds with #6 nostalgia.

Emergency stop! A hen glides into a fishing access beside the East Gallatin, where two cocks peck rose hips under a bush with no leaves. The Brazilian jumps out and locks into willowy posture. But all three birds already up and floating back to private turf. Pow! She swivels and pops off a pine cone in frustration, from 25 yards out. Bonding of the hunting couple.

I watch her lean over as she returns the shotgun to its scabbard in the back of the Cruiser. Those who do not recognize and embrace their weaknesses, immediately, may be condemned to repeat the affairs of the past, slowly.

Certainly, there must be open land somewhere. Topo map consulted. Swatch island of public land discovered. We race there. Pheasants thick but wily, always strutting the private perimeter of the neighbors or sitting on the county road, toeing the stripe with Chinese smiles.

Moral dilemma solved by driving pheasants onto public land, with car and slowly, since roadkill not a sporting method of taking game, whereupon the problem becomes bad shooting by husband. Or, could the gun, so recently and hurriedly purchased, have the wrong choke?

A month ago, I was out in the yard, examining

a Haroldson apple sapling girdled by an angry vole, when the fax rang in the study. I was surprised at the message: "You are meant to understand that if you betray this man's trust in any way you are one dead mangled American—" and so on in less flattering language.

I went to the sheriff, for whom I voted, and not just because he ran unopposed, and he said mine was the first authenticated death threat by fax in the history of the state. An honor, to be sure. I wondered who I could have savaged in recent scribblings.

"Does your dog stray onto other people's property?" asked the sheriff. "Are you a real estate agent? Have you recently sold any property a buyer may not be wholly happy with? What are your views on abortion?" These, said the sheriff, are the most common motivations for death threats in Montana. So much for the enemies of the pen.

"I need," I explained to the clerk at The Bullet Hole, "a gun I can use on intruders and pheasants, both."

He recommended an 870 Express Magnum, and he did not ask how aggressive were the pheasants in my neck of the woods, or whether they communicated by fax. But the only 870 in stock had a duck choke, which holds the shot in a smaller cluster, longer. I only mention these personal details because good guns are supposed to come with emotional baggage. Also, this is what I was thinking about while I missed.

Just then a girl drives up in a Honda, stares at us and at our car, which is in the middle of the road, engine running. I stare at her since, though there is a foot of snow on the ground, her midriff is bare. She's a cheerleader, in cheerleader clothes, coming home from practice.

"Shoot 'em!" says the girl, with a good laugh under a tossing head. "They like to hang in the stubble beyond the barn, by that culvert over there."

Her parents own the adjacent wheat farm, also. We have been Montanan enough to ask. The swirls of pheasant tails are everywhere in the snow, the little foot scratchings, like white tattoos. Call me Ishmael, we eat blubber tonight. The Brazilian can shoot.

Back at the Ipanema Hunt Club, what did they do with the dead pigeons? They plucked them and dressed them and gave them in boxes to the orphanages.

In Montana, we eat like Mandarins.

Kung Pao pheasant. Kung pow, pheasant.

Back shooting again.

Fishing Blind

One day, missing a few and catching some along the grassy green banks of the Yellowstone in Paradise Valley, the guide and I got to trading stories.

The guide told me of floating the summer before with a plucky 82-year-old from California. This old boy was mostly deaf and completely blind. But before his various infirmities had impinged, he had been a very good fisherman. So the guide, whose name is Mac, would call out: "Ten o'clock!" and the man would cast to the left of midnight. "Set!" Mac would then shout, because the old man's cast had been perfect and a trout was taking the fly. The man would raise his rod then, setting the hook. When the trout was tired and close to the boat, Mac would yell, "Now!" and with his free hand the man would follow the bend in his rod to the line and the stretch of his line to the water and the fish's head. The old man would touch the fish with one finger, count time, and smile, and then Mac would take the trout from the hook and let it go, in a swirl of darkness.

I think the old man may be gone now. At least he no longer comes up to Montana to fish. But the image caught hold of me: fishing blind. I had to try it. I don't quite know why.

First, casting, blindfolded. I would go out in the front yard with inner tube targets 20 and 40 feet away in the grass and have my wife, or one of the kids, once they understood the game, shout out distance and angle.

"Nine o'clock! Forty feet!"

The kids moved the targets around and were very careful to make sure I did not peek. I don't know why anglers are suspected of being such cheats.

Soon enough, my flailings improved. I mean, eyes open, I am not a candidate for the winners' circle at the Golden Gate Casting Club. But I didn't snag my own ear lobe, either.

I thought through the problem. What about balance? I would be seated in the drift boat, up front. When the guide saw a rising fish, or a likely spot, I would need to stand up, and quickly lock myself in the braces before casting. For a sighted person, these sculpted half-holes make it easier to hold in the rapids. For me, as with the old man, they would be a necessity. I set out a plastic cooler, this time in the backyard, away from prying eyes. I climbed up the plastic and slipped the bandana over my eyes. Planted my feet wide, rocked this way and that, imagined the rapids and drop-offs of Paradise Valley, which I knew well enough. But try that, eyes closed, standing on a cooler, shooting at silence.

I began to pay more attention to wind, not to the kind that flips the fly wrong, but to the brush of it against my cheek.

There were a few other skills to make the game real. I was persnickety enough to want to try to tie my own flies to the leader. *Make the last loop large, and mark its location with the soft spot between your thumb and forefinger.* Also, I found I kept poking myself with the point of the hook, not out of clumsiness, but from nervous anticipation.

I was ready, but what was I doing this for?

The goofy exercise was making me paranoid. I hoped I wasn't foreshadowing some superstitious accident, setting myself up for a dunking. Like, I lean back around Loch Laven, where the Yellowstone drops 3 to 5 feet down a bar and begins to articulate a bend the cottonwoods call home, and I swipe the July sweat from under the blindfold with my fingers, but these are the fingertips I just brushed a trout's head with, last bend back, so now my eyelids are as greasy as the greasy green Limpopo, with fish sweat, and a damn osprey drops out of the tallest cottonwood I can't see and grabs both my peepers in her hard talons and takes off north to Prometheusville. Something to consider, fishing blind.

So we get to the put in. Mill Creek Bridge. The Gallatins back off to the west like chewed molars. The Absarokas smile down from the east, jagged as a friendly country neighbor's canines. That's just a literary impression. How would I know? My eyes were closed. I was blindfolded with the blue bandanna. I flashed on why the eyes of the condemned are always covered. Nobody wants to chop the head off someone who's staring at them. Executioners hate reprieves.

Anyway, this is about fishing. We shoved off. I decided to start out in the stocks, instead of sitting. That way, I'd already be in position to cast. I trailed my fingers in the water, which I did by bracing myself with my left hand on the lip of the gunwale.

"Muddy in the center," said Mac.

Slug of mud raining down from the Lamar, I guessed. River high enough to push the mud through the first day, still leaves the edges clear as Bombay Sapphire, which is where the fish like to hang. Looks like a big muddy stripe flanked by cleanness, if you have the eyes to see it.

"Three o'clock. Short."

I rode the boat with my knees, like a horse, quick back cast, then quick to 3.

Slack.

"That fish don't like impaired people," says Mac. I thought he might hold the cracks for a few casts, since I was paying him, and Mac seemed to like the old California man.

"What?"

"That brown you just missed don't like—"

"What?"

"You ain't supposed to be deaf, too," says Mac.

"Find us some fish, would you?" I say.

I guess if you really were blind, you'd be most concerned about falling out of the boat. I wasn't that concerned. In the water, I planned to rip the blindfold off, unless a sharp stick poked me in the eye, first. I knew the river between Mill and Pine Creeks. The water only gets deep between the islands close to the Pine Creek Bridge. That would be a bad spot to swim, blind.

"Six o'clock!"

Nailed him. Little guy. Maybe he tail-walked. Maybe he didn't. I waggled him up to the boat, caught the knot of line and leader between thumb and forefinger, slid finger down tippet to feel for the top of his head. The fish swiveled around a bit, but I placed a solid finger kiss on its brain. Live fish head was cold, alien, but fun. I was doing it. I slipped the #12 Trude out of the fish's lip. He was gone.

"That was a rainbow."

"I wouldn't know."

"Yes, you should know, because they pull differently."

It's easy to imagine playing a fish blind. The feel is heightened, there's more suspense, easier to lose 'em. When they're hooked, if they jump, that's bad. You can't see the slack, and you have to make up for that, especially with barbless hooks. You dance. They lead.

Along the Yellowstone, sand-hill cranes sometimes congregate 1000 feet up, long swallowing caws calling the congregation together, little bitty specs, tiny as kingbirds. I don't know why they do that. Sounds like the Marine Corps on tryout day. I've seen it many times. I listened for it, that day. 'Course, it was the wrong time of year.

The mind wanders.

I think you do more remembering blindfolded. I remembered a story my mother told at the dinner my Aunt Susan and my Uncle Jim threw for their fiftieth wedding anniversary. I remembered this because my Aunt Susan went blind last year. My mother, whose name is Dorothy, hid under a blanket in the rumble seat of my Uncle Jim's car, one ancient Sunday when Jim first went sparking with Susan. My mother hid there with her little brother, Uncle John-to-be. This would have been about 1914. They couldn't see a thing, under the blanket. The car stopped. They waited as long as they could. Then they started giggling. Fifty years later, Uncle Jim was still mad they'd followed him into the woods in his own car. He died in 1982. But Uncle John died first, and at little brother John's funeral, Uncle Jim drove to the cemetery, a black Fleetwood, best old man car ever made. Jim ran every red light in Minot, North Dakota, in the Fleetwood, on the way to his brother's grave. He didn't care.

"Jim! Jim! The lights are all red!" My mother yelled from the back seat, a girl again.

"Red lights are a communist conspiracy," said Uncle Jim, running another one. Uncle Jim was strange, for a Republican.

That was a while ago. When Susan went blind, she was 95, advanced middle age in my family, and still cheerful. My mother has never been so cheerful. She always worried about her eyes. Of course, she's only 93, and she can still call the red spot on a sand-hill crane, 60 yards across the pond in front of her house. Then again, a sand-hill is a large bird.

You see your mind, fishing blind, but what I was hearing was the water. Sluicing, thumping, scraping, just the ever-present white noise of its rush. Without the blindfold, the colors masked the sounds. Normally, you'd be looking for a rise, or a little nubbin of a nose behind a rock. The giant TV of the mountains frames you in the boat, and you lose yourself in the visuals, the mountains, those Absarokas, lunging, that sky, you can feel the gradations of blue, unto the ionosphere. Sighted, you don't take note of noise unless it's a rapid calling from around the bend. But sightless, that same rapid takes on menace. How far away is it? How big? Standing waves? With my eyes open, I like to whoop and yell, entering a good rapid. Eyes closed, I shut up, each time we hit some water.

I heard Mac straining. The oars grated in the locks. The drift boat entered a chute. I was trying to figure out where we might be.

"Hold on tight," said Mac.

I smiled. But I was not blind.

"It's dead water all through here," said Mac, after the chute.

"I know."

"What's that?" he asked excited.

It sounded like a goose was about to land on us. Another one. Heavy squawking!

Also, Mac was slapping his hand on the seat, which kind of tipped me off. Our guide was blowing on a duck call. He was laughing pretty hard.

"Want a beer?"

I hesitated.

"Blind people drink," said Mac. "Makes them more sensitive."

"You don't sound sensitive to blind people, Mac."

"You ain't blind," said Mac.

I heard him popping a tab.

"The old man could have had any guide. He always went out with me."

"Maybe I'll take a beer," I said.

We had a couple more.

"Good water," said Mac, after a while. "See, the old man had to do it dark, and you don't."

"We close to the bridge?" I said.

"We're gettin' close to the islands. We're on the right side. By the big rock above the Japanese guy's log house."

"Gotcha."

"They're rising behind the rock, 10 yards. Minimize the drag."

"Angle?"

"One o'clock, sir!"

Hook up this time, and it was a good one. The rod swooped to the gunwale and actually whacked against it, with the force of the strike.

"Pull up!" Mac was shouting.

I threw the rod up like a kid and felt my thighs scrape around in the braces, at the same time as I followed the fish's pull, for my own balance.

"Nice fish!" shouted Mac.

The drag was clicking, starting to scream. This was the first fish to do that all day and, suddenly, I was real excited.

"Yeah!"

"Yeah, fight 'em!"

Fish almost pulled me over. I felt Mac's fingers against mine, loosening the drag. I heard the clunk of him falling back into his seat. Wood against brass, at this point it sounded as if one of his oars had jumped the lock.

"Maybe it's a whitefish," said Mac, once again attempting to toy with me.

"Put the other oar back in the water," I said, from the braces.

There was a clatter. The loose oar must have dropped all the way to the floor.

"Hang on," said Mac. I hate this guy, but I also hate fishing with people who aren't funny.

Unfortunately, it was then that I felt the boat tipping. Water washed over my feet. The boat righted itself, but I could feel we were sideways to the current. I was scared but I didn't think to reach for the blindfold. I wedged myself in the braces and grabbed the gunwale with my left hand as I held tight to the rod with my right. At least the fish was hooked good. It pulled like a kelp bonito from a kayak.

But the drift boat slammed up against something. My butt hit the oar locks. Then I was in the river.

"Throw me the rod!" shouted Mac.

It was not over my head, but it was fast water. I was kind of bouncing along the small rock and gravel bottom, trying to keep my balance. I was not wearing hip boots, thank God. I had the rod in my right hand. I was flailing with the left. The water was warm enough. I've always been amazed how the Yellowstone heats up in the middle of summer, given that it's a mountain river.

"Swim! Swim, man!"

So, I was a little underwater. I'd been in this exact same spot many times before, albeit on the surface. I was not about to let go of the trout.

"Take the blindfold off!"

There was no bottom under me now. But I was floating, somehow, treading water with one arm, slapping the surface with the rod in the other. It oc-

curred to me that I was in the top sweep of an island, being swept around one side, because I was
accelerating and I could hear the suck of water all
around me, whooshing up my ears, as I went under.

I felt a big slap where my neck met my back. Mac
yanked me up by my shirt. He held me against the
side of the boat until the current slowed at the end
of the island.

"Yo, and harken: it's the takeout."

It's a funny feeling being held up in the water by
somebody holding tight to the back of your shirt. I
still had the rod. There wasn't much tug at the end
of the line. I shoved up with my left wrist and pushed
off the blindfold. The unsentimental wonder of what
I saw. Aspens quaking. Canyons running indigo. A
stupid pink cow staring at us from across the river,
spittle on its chin. I was as happy as I'd ever been.
The Pine Creek Bridge was just behind us. We were
eddying out on the left. Mac let go. I touched bottom
with my head above water. I just stood there on the
gravel bottom, my shirt tails floating, and I looked
up at the staircase of greens and blues, trees and
sky, till I caught my breath.

Then I brought in the fish, which was still
hooked. It was a refulgent fat fellow about 19 inches, pretty spent, a cutthroat, orange slash under the
gills, the rising sun, for me. I stared long at those
fishy eyes. Then I let it go.

Fishing blind.

Steve Chapple is the author of eight books and two screenplays. *Kayaking the Full Moon: A Journey Down the Yellowstone River to the Soul of Montana* was chosen as a Notable Book of the Year in the Travel and Science Category by the *New York Times*. It also won a Lowell Thomas Award for best travel book of the year. He co-wrote David Brower's *Let the Mountains Talk, Let the Rivers Run*. A former staff columnist for the *San Francisco Chronicle*, he writes on politics and the environment, adventure and travel for the *New York Times*, the *Los Angeles Times,* the *Christian Science Monitor, National Geographic, Travel & Leisure, Outside, Rolling Stone, Premiere, Audubon, Men's Journal*, and many other magazines. He is a contributing editor of the San Francisco *Examiner* Sunday Magazine and of *Sports Afield*, and the 1997 winner of the Polar-Tek Challenge.

Born at the foot of the Beartooth Mountains in Billings, Montana, and educated at Yale, Chapple currently lives in Bozeman with Brazilian photographer Maria Ines de Pentagna Salgado and their two boys, Cody and Jack.